Contents

FOREWORD

By Bristol Voss

If you have ever been in awe of the whole idea of a three-story-high dump truck or fascinated by the engineering revolution that is speeding mechanical vehicles through the electronic era and into the robotic age, you'll want to grab this copy of *Ultra Haulers*.

Take a seat in your favorite chair and get ready to tour the history, present, and future of the world's greatest haul trucks.

You couldn't have a more qualified, passionate guide to the subject than Mike Woof. As the former editor-in-chief of *World Mining Equipment* magazine, Mr. Woof is a leading authority on mining equipment, easily the only industry that can claim the largest population of actively working, gigantic, land-based hauling machines.

For nearly a decade, Mr. Woof has entertained and informed tens of thousands of loyal readers around the globe with the latest news on the largest, most-sophisticated factory-made equipment produced.

Known for his expert, prescient commentary, he has often been asked—and paid as a consultant—to give his personal opinion on every aspect of these extraordinary vehicles, from what's the biggest, to what makes something the best, and finally to where these machines are headed.

Ultra Haulers will be a distinctive and valuable addition to your library for numerous reasons, but particularly for the scope of the work, its readability, and the fresh perspective that Mr. Woof brings to the material. His deep understanding of the context in which these machines are used and his sympathy for the engineering triumphs they represent—and still face—comes through on every page.

First, Mr. Woof tackles the concept of rigid trucks and delves into the evolution and history of these machines. Next, he follows the path of the articulated dump truck. Mr. Woof makes two necessary detours: first, a brief foray into what many call the key component of these trucks, the tire; and second, a concise briefing on perhaps the most well-known truck manufacturer, Caterpillar. He brings the reader up to date on the very latest refinements to the mega trucks that are working in the field as well as underground, and then concludes with talk of truck advances that sound futuristic—except that they already exist today.

The book incorporates original analysis, primary data, firsthand commentary, and an extraordinary finger on the pulse of a dynamic and exciting field. Both knowledgeable hobbyists and industry veterans will enjoy Mr. Woof's sweeping view, which is beholden to no one manufacturer, no one type of machine, and no one era.

From thesis to substance to style, *Ultra Haulers* is the *ne plus ultra* roundup of the largest and most-sophisticated hauling trucks today.

PREFACE

In writing this book, I've tried to bring together much of the knowledge I gained during my time as editor of *World Mining Equipment* and through my prior experience from the construction field. While some of the information in this book was published in *World Mining Equipment* during my time with the publication, it has never before been brought together in one place and used in this manner to give the reader a logical flow of technical development as it happened historically. The crawler track that established Caterpillar, the rigid truck, and the articulated dump truck (ADT) have been so important to the earthmoving sector that their histories had to be detailed in a manner not recorded previously. In a similar respect, little real attention has been paid to interesting machines like the off-highway tractor, crucial developments such as earthmover tires, or innovations like autonomous machines and radical truck concepts.

ACKNOWLEDGMENTS

I'd like to thank my friends and former colleagues, Kyran Casteel, Dave Porter, Adriana Potts, Jonathan Watt, and Bristol Voss, for their help over the years. Without them, this book would not have been possible. I'd also like to thank my many contacts in the industry, particularly Peter Winkel and Merilee Hunt of Liebherr, Kent Henschen of Bucyrus International, John du Toit at Bell Equipment, and Tracy Burnett at Michelin, for their help in sourcing images for this book.

INTRODUCTION

There have been many books published concerning the histories of various types of off-highway equipment. However, this book plots a different path through the subject, as it investigates certain machines in greater detail and explains some of the technical thinking behind their development. Different types of hauling machines are examined, along with some of their offshoots, key components, and radical developments that have offered a break from proven principles in pointing the way ahead.

Like many other fields of engineering, there have been huge advances made during the last century with earthmoving equipment. This industry has seen true innovators, such as Benjamin Holt, Clarence Best, R. G. LeTourneau, Ralph Kress, the Wagner brothers, and David Brown, build machines that have helped change the way we live. The new technologies these people pioneered have played a major role in building the construction and mining projects that provide the backbone to the developed world. The importance of this heavy machinery is often overlooked but should not be so ignored. Earthmoving equipment has built our cities, towns, roads, and bridges, and has also been used to extract the metals and minerals on which our civilization now relies.

The gulf between the old and the new is vast. Present machines are more productive, more reliable, and offer huge gains in cost per tonne over older designs. While it is easy to admire the durability of the well-engineered and heavily built machines of yesteryear that have survived, it is equally easy to forget that these pieces of equipment are often uncomfortable and tiring to operate for long periods, are comparatively unproductive, and may be unforgiving of the slightest operator error. However, it is only by understanding how these technologies have developed through time that an in-depth knowledge of current machinery can be achieved.

Chapter 1

TRUCK DAWN
EVOLUTION OF THE RIGID DUMP TRUCK

Mechanized mining operations have been revolutionized by the evolution of the rigid truck, providing a cost-effective way to haul dirt around a mine site. These days, the extraction industry relies heavily on truck and shovel/backhoe operation, whether in small quarries or in the largest metal and coal mines. But things were not always so, and the mine truck was not available as mechanized mining began to be employed at the end of the nineteenth century and in the early twentieth century. Instead, operations typically used complex networks of rails, allowing steam locomotives to haul ore wagons to working faces, with loading carried out by steam shovels. This method was successful, though it had limited versatility, as the locomotives were only able to cope with shallow gradients, while their mobility relied on the location of the rails. Track installation was also crucial, and this labor-intensive process, along with frequent derailments, set limits on mine productivity.

With the development of the first crawler tractors by Holt (which merged with archrival Best in 1925 to form Caterpillar), miners had the chance to employ more-mobile machines that could operate without the need for rails. Crawler tractors were used to haul trains of ore carts with metal wheels—a versatile, though relatively slow method. Around the same time, some operations started using conventional commercial road vehicles fitted with truck beds to carry material and loaded these with the early steam-powered cable shovels.

While mechanized digging equipment was developed in the late nineteenth century, earlier methods of muck-shifting persisted well into the twentieth century because of the lack of reliable, self-powered haul trucks, as this image from 1916 shows. *Bucyrus collection*

The birth of the shovel/truck combination provided no golden age for the people who had to use the equipment, though, and this period shouldn't be viewed through rose-tinted eyewear. By modern standards, the trucks were harsh in operation, hard work to drive, unreliable, uncomfortable, and unsafe. Ergonomic design was unheard of, while safety features like seatbelts and effective rollover or falling-object protection were nonexistent. Drivers could count themselves lucky if they had a truck with a canopy to keep the rain off or a padded seat that offered a bare minimum of comfort. Weather protection was minimal, as cabs were generally open and suspension systems were crude, with little in the way of travel or damping. The vehicles vibrated heavily and there was no power steering, so drivers needed arms like weightlifters to cope with a full shift behind the wheel. Because of the constant oscillation, drivers also risked contracting serious vibration white-finger injuries from steering wheels and gear levers. Trucks didn't have electric starters and had to be handcranked, which left many unwary drivers with broken wrists and/or thumbs when engines kicked back—there's a definite knack to handcranking an engine safely, and a moment's inattention can result in painful injury. There were no smooth rides. Seats had minimal padding and were often little more than wooden benches, transferring jolts that the suspension couldn't cope with, as well as engine vibration, straight to the driver's spine.

Early trucks like this Mack offered little in the way of cab comfort, so operators had to provide their own defenses against the elements, though these would have had limited benefit in cold or rainy conditions. *Bucyrus collection*

With little suspension travel, no synchromesh gearboxes, and no power steering, the early trucks were hard work to drive and they were difficult to stop in a hurry because of their minimal brakes. *Bucyrus collection*

The trucks available in 1913 were flimsy affairs, many of which still featured wooden wheels that would splinter under hard use, and these vehicles struggled to cope with site conditions. *Bucyrus collection*

Not only did the basic engineering make life uncomfortable for the driver, but these rickety on-highway vehicles proved too lightly built to cope with the tough conditions, so breakdowns were frequent. Chassis were lightweight, dump bodies had thin sides (often made of wood), and engines and transmissions were feeble and fragile by modern standards.

Some firms tried building curious half-track vehicles to use as haulers in a bid to get around the shortcomings of available tires, but with solid steel wheels at the front, a horizontally mounted steering wheel, and a complete lack of operator protection, this machine must have been hard work to drive. *Bucyrus collection*

Brake systems were marginal even when the vehicles were not loaded, so with a heavy load of dirt in the back, the trucks couldn't be relied upon to stop until they hit something solid. Crude wheel and tire design caused immense problems. A combination of narrow rims and solid tires resulted in limited traction, whether or not twinned wheels were fitted, and trucks would bog down easily in soft ground. Some early trucks even featured wooden rims and/or spokes, which splintered under hard use.

It was in the United States, where volume manufacturing of automobiles first took hold, that development of haul trucks began in earnest. One of the first successful trucks used in mechanized mining and earthmoving operations was the Mack AC, introduced in 1915. The Mack AC wasn't designed specifically for mining, nor was it outstandingly sophisticated compared to other vehicles of the time; its success was linked to its durability, simple layout, and rugged construction. The AC was nicknamed the "Bulldog," due to its characteristically ugly appearance, which resulted from having the radiator mounted between the engine and the cab. As was common on early vehicles, the AC featured chain drive to its rear wheels and was offered with capacities from 7.5–10 U.S. tons/6.8–9 tonnes, while a variety of different bodies could be fitted to the back. However, the original AC suffered from the same shortcomings with regard to solid tires and ineffective brakes as other trucks of the period, though improvements such as pneumatic tires were fitted to later versions. The proximity of the cooling system to the cab also caused safety problems, so drivers had to be wary of being scalded by a burst radiator or of catching a boot in the exposed fanbelt (and possibly losing some toes). The AC's distinct advantage over other machines was that it was far less likely to fall to pieces with the demands of site usage.

The success of the AC made Mack a major player in the off-highway truck market, and over 40,000 rolled off the line during its time in production from 1915 to 1938. The improved Mack AP truck went into production in the early 1930s, and while this retained some of the features of the earlier AC, such as the radiator location and chain drive, it benefited from better chassis, axles, wheels, tires, and brakes. Special versions of the AP were built for off-highway construction and mining duties, and these featured rounded steel bodies and twin axles at the rear, while versions with lightweight aluminum bodies allowed payloads up to 25 U.S. tons/22.7 tonnes.

Also in the United States, C. J. Hug built its H4K in 1926 offering a 3.8-U.S.-ton/3.4-tonne payload, hydraulic tipping, and twinned rear tires, while Lee Trailer and Body

The use of less versatile but reliable rail-based methods for shifting rock continued in many mines and quarries even after trucks became durable enough to haul material dependably, as this image from 1933 shows. *Bucyrus collection*

Conventional on-road vehicles such as this restored Ford Model A truck were fitted with tipping bodies and used for lighter duties on-site.

The use of on-highway trucks in off-highway applications could result in heavy wear and tear, as can be seen in this image from 1939. Missing a door and with no seatbelt to hold the driver in place, this truck would not have passed the most cursory of current safety inspections and its condition would not be acceptable today. *Bucyrus collection*

developed a 1.5-cubic-meter rear-tipping body that could be fitted onto the ubiquitous Ford Model T chassis. Ford's later Model A was also converted for use as a tipper by a wide array of specialist body builders. Because the half-track configuration offered benefits over the shortcomings of available tires in tough road applications, there were a number of attempts to use this layout. One of the most sophisticated was the Lombard half-track of 1927, as it offered a 20-U.S.-ton/18-tonne payload in its 4.6-cubic-meter wooden tipping body, though with solid tires at the front and limited suspension travel from the crawlers at the rear, operator comfort was basic in spite of its enclosed wooden cab.

It was Euclid's Trac-Truk, unveiled in 1933 and widely recognized as the first truck designed exclusively for off-highway use, that proved truly successful in this difficult application. The roots of this truck line began when Euclid Road Machinery was established in July 1931, based in a suburb of Cleveland, Ohio. Like the Mack Bulldog, the Trac-Truk didn't set particular standards for technical innovation other than the fact that, with its reinforced Chevrolet truck chassis and beefed-up components, it was far more heavily built and durable than any truck previously available. With its 7-cubic-yard/5.5-cubic-meter dump body, the Trac-Truk looks small and crude by today's standards, but this machine was the world's first purpose-built dump truck, and it made a huge impact on the earthmoving industry.

As this truck had little in the way of falling object protection for the driver, he showed good common sense in standing out of the cab during loading procedures at this Egyptian cement operation. *Bucyrus collection*

With its solid tires, this Mack offered poor traction in soft ground and would have easily bogged down to its axles in muddy conditions, leaving the operator and other site workers with the problem of having to dig it out again. *Bucyrus collection*

This was the right machine at the right time, as several large construction projects got underway in the United States during this period. The surface mining industry was also increasingly keen to use truck haulage, due in part to the parallel development of effective cable shovels. The Trac-Truk's reinforced, steel-sided body was strong enough to cope with the impact of large rocks, and its hydraulic tipping action was still novel at a time when cable-raise systems were commonplace. Nor had the driver been forgotten, as the Trac-Truk had a canopy that offered some protection from the elements and/or falling rocks. The Trac-Truk could even be fitted with special treads over the rear wheels, so it didn't suffer from a loss of traction on soft and muddy ground like earlier vehicles. Large numbers of these vehicles were used in major construction projects, such as the building of the Hoover Dam.

There was more to come too: a 20-short-U.S.-ton/18-tonne coal hauler version in 1934 and the vastly improved FD Series in 1936. The FD models featured cab protection and reinforced bodies, were powered by Cummins or GM diesels rated at 142 kilowatts/190 horse-power, offered a 15-U.S.-ton/13.5-tonne payload, and were manufactured as late as 1963. It is worth noting, too, that by the mid-1930s, diesels had evolved sufficiently to take the place of the gasoline engines used in early off-highway trucks like the Mack AC. The lower fuel consumption and low maintenance requirements offered by diesels were useful, though the real benefit came from the better torque characteristics.

By now, other firms were looking at this market. Dart built its first off-highway truck in 1937, the same year that Mack introduced its F series. There were a few short-lived firms that entered the market around this time as well, like Trojan Truck Manufacturing and Six Wheels, both of which were based in Los Angeles. Trojan's 1938 machine was of note as it offered a 70-U.S.-ton/63-tonne capacity, making it the world's largest mine truck at the time. Dart went one step further in 1939, offering a diesel-electric

Mack designs evolved over the years, with pneumatic tires replacing the earlier solids and enclosed cabs giving a measure of protection from the environment. *Bucyrus collection*

tractor and bottom-dump trailer unit combination with an 80-U.S.-ton/72-tonne capacity. Diesel-electric drives had been pioneered a few years before in Europe, with U.K. firm Leyland building several models for on-highway use in the early 1930s. This technology was to play a huge role in surface-mine haulage in years to come.

With the Dart, Euclid, and Mack trucks of the late 1930s, the mining industry at last had purpose-built haul trucks that could be relied upon to hold together in tough site conditions, as well as to carry a useful load. Better still, these machines offered a cost/ton ratio for surface mining operations that earlier mechanized mining methods found difficult to match (and mines using railways quickly became rare indeed). Drivers had never had it so good in terms of comfort and safety levels either. Enclosed cabs were more or less standard by now, and pneumatic tires, twinned at the rear, meant that traction was good, while brake, axle, and suspension design had evolved by leaps and bounds. These machines resembled proper haul trucks as they're known today, and it's interesting to note that the origins of some current small quarry trucks can still be seen in Euclid's FD-series machines.

Power was a problem, though, as the engines of the time had output limitations that put a definite cap on payload capacity. Trojan's solution was to use twin engines, and its 70-U.S.-ton/ 63-tonne machine featured two Cat engines delivering 190 horsepower/142 kilowatts (though the firm stopped building trucks in 1942). Euclid followed Trojan's lead by using a twin drive in its FFD machine of 1949. This offered a 34-U.S.-ton/31-tonne payload and featured two Detroit 6-71 engines with separate transmissions for each of its twin axles. Its extra power allowed heavier payloads to be hauled at faster speeds and on steeper grades than had previously been feasible. The quality of engineering reached new highs in the 1940s, spurred on by the needs of the war effort, and this can be seen in how long some of products lasted, both in production and on-site. For example, Mack's simple and rugged L series was introduced in 1940 and remained in production for nearly 20 years. Four- and six-wheeled variants were available and the range included the 34-U.S.-ton/31-tonne-capacity LRVSW and the 40-U.S.-ton/36-tonne-payload LYSW, both of which were powered by 450-horsepower/406-kilowatt Cummins diesels.

1950s, 1960s, and 1970s

While the war years halted the development of nonmilitary products, they heralded major advances in manufacturing technology that were of huge benefit to the engineering industry. This included the off-highway truck sector. The 1950s were a boom period for mining and mining machines, with German firms entering the market with smallish quarry-sized trucks at this time. In 1950, Faun built its K20, a 22-U.S.-ton/20-tonne-payload hauler driven by a 241-horsepower/180-kilowatt diesel, while Kaelble offered a 16 tonner, and in 1951 Südwerke Motoren made the MK15 Cyklop, a 12.5 tonner (later made by Krupp). It was Euclid that really pushed the boundaries, though, when it introduced the 1LLD in 1951. The 1LLD offered a 50-U.S.-ton/45-tonne payload, was driven by twin Cummins engines, and was claimed to be the biggest truck in series production at the time. Dart's Model 75-TA of the same year was bigger still, with a record-beating capacity of 75 U.S. tons/68 tonnes, and also featured twin drive. Although only one was made, the Model 75-TA was interesting for another reason, as it was

By the early 1950s, mines and quarries were able to select a range of reliable and durable trucks from firms like Dart, Euclid, and Mack that could carry a useful payload, such as this twin-engined Euclid 1LLD. *Bucyrus collection*

Euclid was a pioneer with regard to its use of the offset cab layout, now common in the rigid off-highway truck market. However, cab design still had a long way to go in terms of operator comfort and safety protection. *Bucyrus collection*

Post–World War II off-highway trucks were able to benefit from the "trickle-down effect" originating in the rapid pace of engineering development during the pressures of war. *Bucyrus collection*

designed pretty much from the wheels up by Ralph Kress, regarded by many as the "father of the modern mine truck." Kress had worked on off-highway machines before, but the 75-TA was a product of his own ingenuity, and its design pointed the way ahead for many much more successful machines. He went on to work for several other firms, including Caterpillar, LeTourneau-Westinghouse, and his son Ted Kress' company, Kress Corporation. He probably had a greater influence on mine truck design than anyone else in history. Meanwhile, in 1952, the Cline truck range was established by former Dart employee Max Cline, who introduced a 35-U.S.-ton/32-tonne-capacity machine with a three-axle layout. The Cline business continued for many years, but only ever occupied a niche market, while the firm's ownership changed a number of times and the machines were also later sold bearing the Isco name.

Interesting developments were afoot in Japan too, with Komatsu building its first truck, the 15-U.S.-ton/13.5-tonne-payload HD150 in late 1953, which featured a V-shaped body, was powered by a 270-horsepower/200-kilowatt diesel and offered a top speed of 26 miles per hour/42 kilometers per hour. Although the Komatsu engineers had clearly cast critical eyes over the leading machines of the time from Dart, Mack, and Euclid, the rugged HD150 was definitely a Japanese design and heralded more to come. It is also worth remembering that Komatsu beat its present archrival Caterpillar into the off-highway truck sector by nearly 10 years. Euclid Road Machinery changed hands in late 1953 when it was acquired by General Motors, and on January 1, 1954, it was made a division of the group. In 1955, Ralph Kress moved over to Peoria-based WABCO and set about designing a new truck range from scratch. (WABCO had been set up in 1953 when R. G. LeTourneau's equipment interests in Illinois were bought by Westinghouse.) In 1957, WABCO introduced the first machines designed by Kress, a 30-U.S.-ton/27-tonne-payload truck (also available with 20- and 24-tonne payloads) and an 80-U.S.-ton/72-tonne tractor/trailer unit for coal

Truck loading does not necessarily have to be carried out directly by a mining shovel or wheel loader, and there have been interesting departures from the norm developed in the name of efficiency. *Bucyrus collection*

hauling. These set the pattern for the modern mine and quarry hauler. Mr. Kress's WABCO design featured a body configuration that was intended to keep the center of gravity as low as possible so as to maximize stability. The truck also had the now-standard offset cab, which helped keep its wheelbase short, and featured the innovative Hydair hydropneumatic suspension system, which improved its handling ability.

In 1959, R. G. LeTourneau unveiled a diesel-electric truck with a 75-U.S.-ton/70-tonne capacity. (LeTourneau was a far better engineer than he was an accountant, which was why he'd lost control of his Illinois business to Westinghouse and had to switch manufacturing to his operation in Longview, Texas.) At roughly the same time, Unit Rig lifted the covers from its prototype M-64 Lectra-Haul, which also had an electric drive. The LeTourneau and Unit Rig machines attracted interest, but it was Mack's M series that attracted sales. The M-series machines were offered with single and twin axles and

The first purpose-built diesel/electric-drive mine trucks from LeTourneau, Unit Rig, and WABCO appeared in the late 1950s and early 1960s. By 1968, when this image was taken, technical development had made it possible for such trucks to achieve payloads in excess of 120 U.S. tons/109 tonnes. *Bucyrus collection*

By the early 1970s, coal stripping methodology was well established with techniques comparable to the present day. The proven loading and hauling machinery used by most large mines was, however, comparatively small. *Bucyrus collection*

The length of coal haulers restricts their use to sites with relatively level haul roads, and ramps have to be designed carefully with gradual gradients. *Bucyrus collection*

replaced the tried-and-trusted L series, but the M-series machines retained the rugged and durable construction of their predecessors.

Meanwhile, payloads continued to grow, thanks mainly to new and more powerful twin-axle tractor units towing increasingly larger trailers (not all of which featured the bottom-dump configuration for coal hauling). Euclid's twin-power Model 50FDT had offered a 50-U.S.-ton/45-tonne payload from 1948 on and was followed by a repowered 1LLD in 1958 that carried a creditable 150 U.S. tons/135 tonnes in its rear-dump trailer. Dart's Model 50S-BDT of 1953 offered a 60-U.S.-ton/55-tonne capacity in its bottom-dump trailer, while the 95EDT of 1960 offered a 95-U.S.-ton/86-tonne payload and featured a rear-dump configuration. M-R-S had been buildng tractor units since the early 1940s, and the largest of these offered payloads up to 50 U.S. tons/45 tonnes by the 1950s.

Double-sided loading, as with this Bucyrus shovel and Caterpillar and Euclid haul trucks, offers an effective production technique and was pioneered many years ago. *Bucyrus collection*

(Caterpillar had been making wheel tractors since the early 1940s, and though these were designed initially for pulling scraper boxes, wagons for hauling dirt were also available.)

Around this time, several other firms were also entering the market. International started making off-highway trucks in 1957, while BelAZ in Belarus offered its first truck, the 28-U.S.-ton/25-tonne-capacity MAZ-525, in 1958 and began selling units to Soviet-Block countries as well as to Egypt, China, and India. In this same year, the U.K. firm Aveling-Barford introduced its 30-U.S.-ton/27-tonne and 35-U.S.-ton/32-tonne SN series, the first in a long line of haulers from the company. Also in the U.K. were firms like AEC and Scammell, though these companies concentrated mainly on ruggedized versions of on-highway trucks. British firm Foden's FR6 was a proper 28-U.S.-ton /25.4-tonne-capacity quarry/mine truck though, with power from a 400-horsepower/300-kilowatt Rolls-Royce diesel, while Heathfield began making small quarry-sized trucks. One of the biggest trucks of this period was the French firm Berliet's T100, powered by a 30-liter

V-12 delivering 970 horsepower/720 kilowatts through an eight-speed gearbox and which ran on three axles, claiming a 111-U.S.-ton/100-tonne payload.

During the 1960s, payload capacities began to rise at an almost unprecedented rate, thanks largely to technological improvements in engine design, and this process paved the way for the much larger mining operations that are now commonplace around the world. LeTourneau's curious three-wheeled, diesel-electric TTR60 of 1960 was interesting, as it offered a 60-U.S.-ton/54-tonne payload and was driven by an 1,130-horsepower/840-kilowatt diesel, though this machine was not exactly a high-volume seller. More down-to-earth was the 1960 launch from BelAZ, its three-axle MAZ 530 with a 45-U.S.-ton/40-tonne payload, and in the same year the company also rolled out its 1,000th MAZ 525. Then BelAZ produced the significantly more advanced 540 prototype (with a 30-U.S.-ton/27-tonne capacity) in 1961. Caterpillar entered the off-highway-truck sector during the early 1960s and quickly made its mark in the industry. In 1962, Caterpillar unveiled its first proper

Modern mining methods use fleet management software to optimize truck scheduling so that an empty truck rolls up to the loading machine as the previous hauler is filled, although such technology was undreamed of until computers became widely available. *Bucyrus collection*

truck, the ubiquitous 769, with a 35-U.S.-ton/32-tonne payload and mechanical drive allowing a travel speed of 42 miles per hour/66 kilometers per hour. Although it was small even by the standards of the day and aimed mainly at construction or quarrying duties, the 769 set a pattern for Cat's entire truck line that continues through to the present giant mining machines.

Euclid was to set a record in 1962 by winning an order for 142 trucks for a dam construction project in Pakistan. And with subsequent orders for more machines, Euclid eventually supplied 250 trucks in all for this project.

Italian firm Perlini also made its first prototype dump truck around this time, introducing a line of 17–32-U.S.-ton/15–29-tonne-capacity machines soon after. Then in 1963, Unit Rig's 85-U.S.-ton/77-tonne-capacity M-85 Lectrahaul (with a diesel-electric drive) appeared as a production model, while International started building 45-U.S.-ton/41-tonne-capacity machines with all-wheel

drive. The Unit Rig M-85 was of particular significance as it was the first diesel-electric machine to go into series production. (The impact of Cat's 769 should need no explanation.) Though it wasn't the first diesel-electric truck by any means, the M-85's success paved the way for these drive systems in the mining industry, as well as marking the end of the line for trucks with maintenance-intensive, twin mechanical drives. Also in 1963 appeared the prototype BelAZ 548, which would set a trend in the Soviet Block for truck design in coming years. Caterpillar was keen to expand its truck line, too, and at the same time as it was building its first batch of 769s, the company hired the redoubtable Mr. Kress, who set about designing the firm's first range of diesel-electric machines. Caterpillar's 75-U.S.-ton/68-tonne-payload 779 with its twin axles, and the 100-U.S.-ton/91-tonne-payload 783 prototypes with three axles, front and rear steering, and DC drive in the middle, were ready for testing by 1964.

The development of haul-truck technology can be seen clearly in dump-body design, with sloping floors that help prevent load spillage on rough ground and also allow for more even material dumping during tipping. *Bucyrus collection*

In many ways, 1965 was a landmark year for the off-highway truck industry, as it marked a time of rapid expansion, and not just in the United States. BelAZ put its 30-U.S.-ton/27-tonne-capacity 540 model into series production, while WABCO was offering the 120A with electric rear drive and power from a 930-horsepower/839-kilowatt diesel. During 1965, Euclid rolled out its innovative R-X prototype, which featured payloads of 85 or 105 U.S. tons/77 or 95 tonnes, depending on engine power, articulated chassis, twin tires, and all-wheel steer. Also that year, the Kress Corporation was established by Ralph Kress's son Ted. There was the short-lived T-65 from Clark Equipment's Michigan subsidiary (better known for its wheel loaders), with a 65-U.S.-ton/60-tonne payload, twin axles, and mechanical drive. Around this time, Dart broke an important barrier by building the first mechanical-drive truck that could carry more than 100 U.S. tons/91 tonnes on two axles with its D-2771, while BelAZ began making its 40-U.S.-ton/36 tonne 548A in 1966.

The late 1960s were a time of increasing change, both in terms of world events and for the truck sector too. Although Caterpillar's electric-drive 779 was made available from 1967 and was followed by the 100-U.S.-ton/91-tonne-capacity 783 and the 786, a 240-U.S.-ton/216-tonne coal hauler in 1968, these Kress-designed machines were perhaps too innovative for the available technology. The 783, with its curious front/rear steering, center-drive layout, and side-tipping body, was certainly interesting technically but did not prove to be a success. A small fleet of the 786 coal haulers was built for the Captain Mine in Illinois, and these machines were powered by engines fitted at either end, running on four axles and twinned tires. Like the 783, this design proved a disappointment. The 75-U.S.-ton/68-tonne-capacity 779 was by far the most orthodox of the Caterpillar electric trucks in terms of design, but even this machine failed to excite the market. In fact, Caterpillar axed its electric-drive truck models in 1969 and bought back the units in the field, opting instead to focus on

Draglines have long been among the largest machines used in coal mining. This image from 1969 is deceptive, as the dragline is Big Muskie, the biggest dragline ever built, so it is no surprise that the loading and hauling equipment looks small in comparison. *Bucyrus collection*

For loading, it is not always necessary to have the truck and shovel operating at the same level, but this can make bucket dumping difficult and may result in more spillage. *Bucyrus collection*

Because of the low specific density of coal, high-volume bodies can be used, as on this LectraHaul machine. Although the coal is relatively light, the bodies still have to be designed carefully to keep the center of gravity as low as possible and prevent the truck's stability from being compromised. *Bucyrus collection*

mechanical-drive machines. Caterpillar's 50-U.S.-ton/45-tonne 773 appeared in 1970 and used a mechanical driveline that followed the pattern set by the 769.

Unit Rig's LectraHaul M-200 of 1968 had a 200-U.S.-ton/181-tonne capacity and a laden weight of 344 U.S. tons/310 tonnes, putting it into the record books of the time. But because of the truck's size, finding a suitable engine was a problem, and Unit Rig elected to power the machine with a two-stroke locomotive diesel that delivered 2,212 horsepower/1,650 kilowatts at 900 rpm, although it had the

double disadvantage of being both heavy and thirsty. This, along with tire-life problems in the hot running conditions of U.S. mines in southwestern states, limited its impact, and it would be three years before a more reliable solution for payloads of this scale would come to market. Meanwhile in Europe, Perlini introduced the T40 in 1968, a 45-U.S.-ton/40-tonne quarry truck with a 590-horsepower/440-kilowatt Detroit Diesel engine, while Faun's K40 came out in the same year with a similar payload, driven by a 536-horsepower/400-kilowatt Deutz diesel.

Caterpillar may have been a late entrant in the rigid truck sector, but it has since come to dominate the market with its mechanical-drive machines. *Bucyrus collection*

The KL2450 was the first of the 240-U.S.-ton/216-tonne-class trucks and was on the market nearly 10 years before rival firms had competing designs ready. Although KL2450 001 is now on display in a museum, some of the other early Wiseda machines are still in use. *Liebherr collection*

Also in 1968, legal issues came to bear as the U.S. courts had decided that GM's ownership of Euclid gave it too strong a share of the truck market. This development provided a cash injection for the legal profession, and the firm was forced to sell its U.S. Euclid truck manufacturing facility to White, kicking off a confusing and complex ownership merry-go-round for the Euclid and Terex brands that would continue for many years. While GM was allowed to retain the factory it owned in Scotland, it had to market those products (scrapers and dozers as well as trucks) separately, and as a result introduced its new Terex brand. Then in 1969, BelAZ put its 83-U.S.-ton/75-tonne-capacity 549 (first seen in prototype form the year before) into series production, while Ralph Kress moved to the firm controlled by his son, Ted, and started working on coal hauler designs. Around that period, other European firms entered the dump truck market with small, conventional, mechanical-drive machines, most notably Kockums in Sweden with its Scania diesel-powered LT-18, followed by the larger LT-2A, 420, 424, and 425 models.

The 1970s were an interesting time, technically, and the new truck designs started with Aveling Barford's Centaur range in 1970. At roughly the same time, Euclid also set up a deal with Brugeoise et Nevelles in Belgium to produce Euclid trucks for the European market. Then in 1971, dump trucks began making headlines thanks to radical jumps in payload capacity and the use of revolutionary drive systems. Ralph Kress' "unitized" coal haulers offered 150-U.S.-ton/135-tonne payloads, and the rear-mounted engine supplied direct mechanical drive to the twin rear wheels. Moreover, the twinned front wheels could be turned by 90 degrees, allowing a Kress coal hauler to turn, more or less, in its own length. These machines were much-improved versions of the 786 model that Kress had developed for Caterpillar, and as he'd learned some valuable engineering lessons, the Kress coal haulers soon proved successful in a niche application.

WABCO's 3200 truck went one stage further in terms of capacity and offered an initial payload of 200 U.S. tons/180 tonnes (later increased to 250 U.S. tons/225 tonnes for the 3200B). This truck featured a novel tandem

This three-axle Foden truck was simple in design, extremely durable, and long-lived, though the U.K. firm opted out of the off-highway market and chose to concentrate on its successful on-/off-highway tipper trucks instead.

electric drive at the rear, with 2,000 horsepower/1,490 kilowatts available from its heavyweight locomotive engine. There was also the curious yet innovative V-Con prototype from Peerless Manufacturing, which offered a 260-U.S.-ton/234-tonne payload and again used a heavy, low-speed locomotive engine (this time supplied by Alco) that delivered 3,000 horsepower/2,237 kilowatts. With four pairs of wheels, the V-Con's unusual chassis design meant that right and left sides of the truck could flex independently, which must have been unnerving for the driver. Despite its initial promise, the machine never made it beyond prototype testing, and although Marion bought the rights to the design and offered various models, none made it into production.

Even more innovative was Euclid's R210 of 1971, which took a different approach to the power limitations of available high-speed diesels by employing an 1,850-horsepower/1380-kilowatt gas turbine from Avro-Lycoming. Like the firm's earlier R-X, the R210 had four-wheel-drive and steered by means of its articulated chassis. Interestingly, Belarus-based BelAZ also announced a gas turbine

The Scandinavian Kockums line was absorbed into the Euclid lineup and later dropped, though versions were also made under license in Brazil by Randon, which has continued to improve the designs.

Aveling Barford's rigid trucks first appeared in the 1950s and were developed continuously, proving particularly successful in the U.K. quarrying sector. The RD65 was the top-of-the-range machine, with a planned 85 tonner never progressing further than its chassis construction.

prototype a short while later that featured articulated frame steering, 4WD, and had a similar payload. After an initial fanfare, little more was heard about this machine, though the articulated frame configuration was to be used in a later BelAZ design.

Although Euclid's R210 was an innovative concept, tests soon began to show what automotive companies that had tested gas turbines in cars, such as Rover, had already found out. While gas turbines are a good power solution for aviation needs, they're not so suitable for cars or trucks for a number of reasons. Gas turbines generate huge quantities of heat energy so they have to be built from expensive titanium or Nimonic alloys that can cope with the temperatures. Steel is not suitable, as it loses its mechanical strength under the temperatures gas turbines generate, so these engines can't be made cheaply if they're going to last more than a few operating hours. In practice, the R210 proved noisy and thirsty, while the prospect of field maintenance to replace costly titanium or Nimonic alloy internals was more or less out of the question. There was also the issue of safety, and given the volatile nature of jet fuel, it's unlikely a gas turbine–powered vehicle would have been able to meet the mining legislation that would come in years following. Truck fires are dangerous enough when they occur on conventional diesel-powered machines, but the prospect of providing sufficient cooling for a hot turbine and shielding the jet fuel tanks in the event of fire breaking out would have posed a major engineering challenge.

By comparison, the announcements in 1971 of the new Rimpull truck business in Olathe, Kansas, and GM's diesel-electric Terex 33-15 prototype with a 150-U.S.-ton/135-tonne payload were fairly low-profile developments in the same year that the R210 was introduced. While it may not have seemed so at the time, the 33-15 was a more important milestone than the technological blind alley represented by Euclid's R210. In 1972, GM's four-year ban from selling off-highway trucks had ended, and the firm began marketing the Terex 33-15, which was to be followed by another six size classes in the coming years. These ranged from the tiny 33-03, with a 22-U.S.-ton/20-tonne payload, up to the 33-19, which offered a 350-U.S.-ton/316-tonne capacity that would not be surpassed for over 20 years. This last machine, the Terex Titan, was a monster,

Aveling Barford's 44-U.S.-ton/40-tonne-payload RD44 introduced in 1998 was the last new model in the range, as the firm found competition tough and eventually pulled out of the rigid truck sector.

powered by a huge locomotive engine that delivered 3,300 horsepower/3,000 kilowatts and featured four electric-wheel motors at the rear. Running on three axles, the truck had a novel rear-steer system designed to reduce tire scrubbing at the back. Given the quantum leap in payload it offered, it's understandable that this huge machine attracted enormous interest at the time. But the truck weighed over 256 U.S. tons/231 tonnes unladen, and because of its sluggish acceleration and enormous fuel consumption at a time of escalating fuel prices (thanks to the oil crisis of the period) it was not cost-efficient to run. Although the prototype machine was used in Canada for many years, only one Terex Titan was ever built. It is now displayed in a mining museum.

Euclid was keeping up the pressure on the truck market, setting up its plant at Guelph, Ontario, to build 75–85-U.S.-ton/68–77-tonne-capacity trucks for Canadian customers as well as overseas markets. For 1974, Euclid launched its R170. With diesel-electric drive, it was a rather more-conventional machine than the experimental

R210. Not surprisingly, this 170-U.S.-ton/153-tonne-payload truck soon proved highly successful for the firm and was to lead to larger machines built along similar lines.

On a smaller scale, the Brazilian firm Randon first moved into the rigid-truck sector in the same year, when it signed a license deal with Swedish company Kockums. This agreement allowed Randon to build a version of the Kockums 424 quarry truck for the Brazilian market and for export to some other South American countries. Caterpillar's 1975 introduction of the 777 made few headlines compared with the Terex Titan slightly earlier. However, like Terex's 33-15 a few years earlier, which initially had been overshadowed by Euclid's R210 but eventually proved to be a milestone, Cat's 777 was a landmark machine. It had a far greater impact on the market than Terex's Titan, which was akin to a dinosaur and doomed to extinction almost from the moment it rolled out of the factory. Initially offering an 85-U.S.-ton/77-tonne payload, the 777 was the firm's first mine-sized truck

The unitized Kress coal haulers have rear-mounted engines and are designed as bottom dumps only. Their novel steering systems allow small turning radii, as this CH300 shows. *Dave Porter*

and quickly became popular on surface-mining sites—as is the current model today. The 777 heralded further developments from Caterpillar and prompted rival firms to build competing units. The Rimpull range also evolved during this time, featuring mechanical drives and offering rear-dump models with payloads of 60–120 U.S. tons/50–110 tonnes and tractor/bottom-dump units with capacities of 100–170 U.S. tons/91–153 tonnes. Technological development was not limited to the United States either, as BelAZ broke the 122-U.S.-ton/110-tonne barrier with its 7519 rear-dump truck, setting the pattern for future designs.

Meanwhile, Euclid had once again changed hands and was sold to Daimler-Benz in 1977, heralding a spate of sales and acquisitions in the off-highway truck sector. The 1970s were a time in which firms developed the coal hauler concept, with WABCO, Unit Rig, and the short-lived Goodbary company all producing machines that followed the lead set by Kress. Goodbary's 100–170-U.S.-ton/91–153-tonne trucks had a similar frame layout

The Terex R-series trucks shared design features with the Euclid R series, due to the links that existed between these firms, although these ties ended when Euclid was sold.

Repowering trucks offers a new lease of life, and this tired old Terex machine was waiting for a new engine and a rebuild before being sent on to a mining operation.

to the Kress machine, with electric drive at the rear and engines at the front. By comparison, WABCO's Coalpak had a 170-U.S.-ton/153-tonne payload, an engine at the back, and electric drive. Unit Rig's first bottom dump was the BD-145, a 145-U.S.-ton/131-tonne-capacity machine with a rigid chassis that was then redesigned as the BD-30 with the same payload.

1980s–Present

Just as the 1960s and 1970s were times in which truck payloads first doubled, then tripled, the 1980s were synonymous with a rapid spate of acquisitions as a hard-nosed approach to the manufacturing business took hold. The decade started with a recession, which put pressure on the mining industry and the equipment suppliers. Dart's 2085 coal truck of 1980 was interesting, as it was the world's largest-ever tandem-axle truck, but its 85-U.S.-ton/77-tonne payload was nothing new technologically. Mack's last designs for the dump truck market had not been a success, and the firm opted to pull out of the off-highway

hauler sector around that time, focusing instead on its on-highway machines.

At that point, the buyouts started in earnest, with the ill-fated IBH Group buying Terex from GM in 1981. IBH expanded at an impressive speed by buying up a series of smaller off-highway equipment firms, including U.K. excavator firm Hymac and German excavator, dozer, and wheel loader company Hanomag, to name but a few. Many of these made competing products, such as the Hymac and Hanomag excavators and Terex and Hanomag wheel loaders. And, while there was some badging, there was little coordinated effort made to streamline the product line. The IBH Group grew too fast and quickly developed serious financial problems that brought about its collapse in 1983 (the head of the firm then served time in prison for IBH's financial irregularities). Terex continued in business, though, first bought back by GM and then sold to Northwest Engineering in 1986. (Hymac was sold twice and then disappeared in the early 1990s, while Hanomag was bought by Komatsu in 1989.) Based in Canada, the

When Liebherr bought out Wiseda in 1995, it redesigned the truck line with the improved T262 taking over from the KL2450, which had started the 240-U.S.-ton/216-tonne class in the early 1980s. *Liebherr collection*

Northwest Engineering group bought Unit Rig in 1988, though the Northwest name was subsequently dropped and the firm continues today as the Terex Corporation, now based in the United States. Dart had been passed around from one owner to another over the years but in 1984, the firm was bought by Unit Rig; so, by 1988 the Terex, Unit Rig, and Dart truck lines were all part of the same group. (In the late 1990s, Terex also added the Payhauler truck range, developed initially by International, to its lineup and more recently bought out the old Kaelble truck/loader business in Germany.)

During the financial disaster that destroyed IBH, GM kept hold of the Terex Titan division in Ontario that made the 33-15 (and developed the huge 33-19) but then sold this operation to LeTourneau in 1985. The original 33-15 design had already been upgraded a couple of times under GM ownership and had developed into the 170-U.S.-ton/153-tonne-capacity 33-15C by the time the range was bought by LeTourneau. The 33-15C continued to be improved under LeTourneau's direction and was developed into the T-2000 range in 1987, with payloads of 170–200 U.S. tons/153–180 tonnes.

In the early 1980s, Clark-Michigan re-entered the mine truck business by buying Euclid from Daimler-Benz, and in 1984 the firm set up a joint venture with Volvo in Sweden, establishing Volvo-Michigan-Euclid (VME). Also in 1984, WABCO was bought by Dresser Industries, and in 1988 Dresser set up a joint venture with Komatsu for the mining and construction equipment markets. The WABCO name was then dropped, though it is still used as a generic term by some miners.

One of the relatively few notable technological innovations for the dump truck market during this period of rapid-fire acquisitions was the 1982 launch of Wiseda's 220-U.S.-ton/200-tonne machine at the MINExpo exhibition in Las Vegas. The truck attracted a great deal of attention, not the least of which was because it had been developed by a nearly unheard-of newcomer to the business. Wiseda was named after its owner, William Seldon Davis, and many wise voices were quoted as saying that such a large truck would never catch on—the V-Con and Terex Titan certainly hadn't—and that if Davis' idea was such a good one, why hadn't the likes of Euclid or Unit Rig thought of it first? Built in the one-horse town of Baxter Springs, Kansas (best known beforehand as a fuel stop on the famous Route 66 and as the scene of one of Jesse James' bank robberies in the nineteenth century), the Wiseda KL-2450 was offered with a choice of Cummins, Detroit, or MTU engines rated at 2,000 horsepower/1500 kilowatts. More was to come, and the KL-2450 (which, oddly enough, is reputed to have received its nomenclature from a Baxter Springs phone number) was soon uprated in payload capacity to the now standard 240-U.S.-ton/216-tonne class. Sales were slow at first, but Wiseda supplied several units in the United States and Australia, and these machines developed a reputation for longevity, which caused other manufacturers to begin to take note. In fact, the first Wiseda truck, 001, only stopped operating a few years ago, having clocked some 100,000 hours in a Minnesota taconite mine, and this machine is now preserved in a local museum. (The 002 through 006 Wiseda units were still running at the time of writing; all had topped 100,000 hours and some were heading for 120,000 hours.)

The Euclid name was to be seen on a new truck in 1985, with the appearance of the R190, a 190-U.S.-ton/171-tonne hauler that followed the firm's now-established diesel-electric-drive layout and was an evolution of its existing range. Unit Rig's BD-240 of 1986 may have matched the payload of Wiseda's KL-2450, but the Unit Rig truck was a bottom-dump coal hauler—the biggest one of its time—with the familiar tractor/trailer configuration. The BelAZ 75211 of 1983 offered a 190-U.S.-ton/170-tonne payload (later increased to 222 U.S. tons/200 tonnes in some duties) and showed the firm was serious about offering bigger trucks, while the firm also notched up its 1,000th 83-U.S.-ton/75-tonne 549. And while Caterpillar's steady introduction of ever-larger mechanical-drive trucks during the 1980s was interesting, this was evolutionary rather than revolutionary. Cat offered the 150-U.S.-ton/135-tonne-capacity 785 in 1985 and followed it with the 190-U.S.-ton/171-tonne-payload 789 in 1988.

It wasn't until the late 1980s and early 1990s that other manufacturers developed prototypes and were then able to offer true production machines matching the

Hitachi bought 100 percent of Euclid when it bought Volvo's remaining share of the business in the late 1990s. The Euclid name was dropped a few years after the purchase, and the machines now have the Hitachi brand. *Jonathan Watt*

This Unit Rig had spent much of its working life in the balmy climate of southern Spain before being shipped off to the colder climes of northern Sweden, although the machine needed little modification despite the different operating temperatures.

payload of Wiseda's KL-2450 (and later, beating that of the old Terex Titan). LeTourneau's Model T-2240, Dresser's Haulpak 830E, and Cat's 793 all rolled out of the various factories in quick succession, and the "experts" who'd questioned Wiseda's logic in developing the KL-2450 were forced to eat their words.

The 1990s were a time when firms again started pushing the boundaries of rigid-truck payload, with BelAZ in Belarus making the first step by offering a 310-U.S.-ton/280-tonne-capacity truck in 1990. Its 7550 utilized a similar articulated frame concept as the one tried on the firm's gas-turbine prototype of the 1970s, and this behemoth was now powered by a locomotive engine, with twinned tires and DC drives giving all-wheel drive. A fleet of 7550s was built, and these have been operated for some years in a Russian mine, though the model is no longer available. The 7550 earned its place in the history books as the first series-produced "ultra hauler," as this size class has

since become known in the industry. However, whether the machine was ever truly cost-effective is a subject open to debate. The firm even showed its improved 7570 concept at the MINExpo 2000 exhibition, but this design never even reached the prototype stage, and BelAZ's biggest truck at present is the 222–244-U.S.-ton/200–220-tonne-capacity 7530, offered with a choice of Cummins QSK60, Detroit Diesel/MTU 16V4000, or Yamz engines rated in the 3084–2661 horsepower/2,300–2,400-kilowatt range.

Coal hauler development had continued too, with Rimpull introducing a 280-U.S.-ton/253-tonne-capacity bottom-dump tractor/trailer combination with mechanical drive in 1990. The firm also developed novel tandem trailer units with 270-U.S.-ton/243-tonne capacities and 1,500-horsepower/1353-kilowatt mechanical-drive axles around the same time. In 1994, Kress' CH300 became the largest unitized hauler ever built. The three machines bought by Coteau Properties in North Dakota in 1995

The rear axle of Caterpillar's 797/797B retains the firm's trademark mechanical driveline system and features a huge differential. Although it is large, this differential follows the same basic design principles as seen in the firm's first haul truck, the 769, launched in the early 1960s.

offered 300-U.S.-ton/270-tonne payloads initially (now upgraded to 340 U.S. tons/308 tonnes, according to the latest Kress information). The CH300s were powered by Cat 3516 diesels and featured improved versions of the innovative suspension, drive, and steering systems that Kress had used on its bottom-dump haulers since it launched the CH150.

Early in 1995, Unit Rig announced its MT4400, which could carry up to 260 U.S. tons/239 tonnes, depending on body plating (though it was really a 240-U.S.-ton/216-tonne machine that competed with Cat's 793, Komatsu's 830E, LeTourneau's T2240, and the original Wiseda KL-2450). That same year, Liebherr made an important step into the dump truck business by buying Wiseda, but it was Komatsu Dresser's Haulpak 930E that really set things going when it was announced in June 1995 and shown to the industry at large at MINExpo in September 1996.

The 930E (so called because its original design GVW was 930,000 pounds, though the prototype was actually heavier) became the first of the commercially successful ultra class of trucks to see the light of day (the BelAZ 7550 was only produced in small numbers and was dropped from the range some years ago). The prototype was powered by an MTU engine, though production versions had first the new Detroit Diesel 16V4000 power unit and then later switched to Komatsu/Cummins power. What really set the 930E apart, though, was its use of an AC drive instead of the DC systems that had been used until then. GE and Haulpak had developed this drive jointly, with its integral wet-plate brakes, and it was the use of the AC system that permitted the 930E's 280–310-U.S.-ton/253–280-tonne payload (soon increased to 320 U.S. tons/290 tonnes). Not far from the Haulpak 930E on the Komatsu stand at the 1996 MINExpo exhibition was the Hitachi Euclid booth and the R260—with a payload of 260 U.S. tons/239 tonnes, it was also the first in a new line. Although the R260 had a DC drive, it was basically the prototype for the firm's 280-U.S.-ton/254-tonne-payload R280AC, which began tests shortly after (and an improved and further extended version of the chassis is now used in Hitachi's top-of-the-line EH5000). Several R260s were manufactured and operated too, so this was by no means a one-off unit, and although the build run was comparatively short, a number of mines were equipped with this machine. Liebherr's new truck for this exhibition was the KL-2420, though with its 190-U.S.-ton/171-tonne payload it competed with the Haulpak 730E and Caterpillar 789 and didn't set any capacity records. Not to be outdone, Caterpillar placed a sign on a 793 at MINExpo 1996 exhibition showing that the truck could carry up to

260 U.S. tons/234.5 tonnes in certain duties where body wear plating could be minimized.

Although LeTourneau continued to offer trucks into the mid-1990s, the firm stopped progressive development of this product line and its mining equipment focus now centers on developing its highly successful large wheel loaders instead. The LeTourneau trucks were still available on request for a period, but apart from a few concept sketches for a large machine with three axles called the Titan 3320, no new models were developed. These design drawings resembled the Terex 33-19, and presumably this would have featured modern engine and drive technology—LeTourneau hinted that it had a novel solution to the ultra hauler concept—but the project appears to have been shelved.

Since Komatsu unveiled the 930E, all the other major manufacturers have offered their own ultra-class machines.

Caterpillar's 797, seen here at the firm's Tinaja Hills proving ground near Tucson, Arizona, was developed primarily to meet the needs of Canada's tar sands industry. However, the machine has also sold well into large coal mining operations in the United States and Australia.

Huge improvements in design have resulted in machines that are more comfortable, safer, and less physically demanding to operate.

Unit Rig's MT3300 was one of the first trucks to be offered with the MTU4000- series engine and was later the first mine truck outside of the ultra hauler class to be offered with AC drive.

The evolution of these trucks can be traced in a straight line from Kress' 1957 WABCO design. Caterpillar has its 797, now available as the revised 797B with a payload of 345 tonnes and power from a 3524B diesel (basically, two 3512s joined crankshaft to crankshaft). Cat's 797/797B is of note as it is the only ultra truck to use a mechanical drive rather than an AC electrical system. Hitachi, which now owns Euclid, has its EH4500 (the upgraded R280AC) as well as the all-new EH5000, with a 290-U.S.-ton/320-tonne payload, power from Detroit's 16V4000 (a Cummins engine is also offered), and a Siemens AC drive. Liebherr's T282 also uses a Siemens AC drive, and this truck has the biggest payload of them all. The improved T282B has a payload of 400 U.S. tons/360 tonnes and power from either the Cummins QSK60, QSK78, or Detroit 20V4000. Unit Rig's revised MT5500B grew out of the MT4800 concept and was first seen in the metal as the MT5500. Now upgraded as the MT5500B, the Unit Rig machine offers a 360-U.S.-ton/325-tonne payload, while its AC drive is supplied by General Atomics, and it has the same customer options for engines as Liebherr's T282B. Liebherr has also built its innovative TI272, a 320-U.S.-ton/290-tonne-payload truck developed out of a concept suggested originally by mining firm BHP. The TI272 (or ILMT as it was first known) is still being tested and features a unique rear drive, rear suspension, and chassis layout that reduces its unladen weight considerably in comparison with conventional designs. However, Liebherr says that the truck is not ready for the market at this stage. BelAZ has now set up a deal with Siemens that will result in its re-entering the ultra hauler sector too, with power from a Cummins diesel as the engine company has an existing engine-supply agreement with the Belarussian firm. Its 75600 will be a 354-U.S.-ton/320-tonne-payload machine, and at the time of writing the machine was due for introduction in 2008.

These ultra haulers are not the same, though. Apart from the differences in power transmission to the rear wheels, such as the different wheel-motor suppliers or mechanical driveline used by Caterpillar, the machines are built along different lines. A good example of this is with the front suspension configurations. Caterpillar's 797B uses a strut-type suspension, a beefed-up version of the system the

company has used on all of its rigid haulers. Liebherr takes a very different approach, with a double-wishbone setup, while Unit Rig fits a sturdy beam axle.

It is worth noting, though, that Caterpillar, Hitachi, Komatsu, Liebherr, and Unit Rig have not been developing these giant trucks in a vacuum, simply because modern technology makes them feasible and the firms hope that customers will buy the machines as soon as they become available. All the firms have been responding to a need to reduce haulage costs in large mining applications by increasing the scale of the equipment used over many years, and the ultra trucks represent the latest stage in this trend. Perhaps more importantly, the ultra trucks also meet a request from mining firms that are finding it harder and

The EH1700 was one of the revamped models launched just after Hitachi took full control of the Euclid business, and this truck was aimed at the 100-U.S.-ton/91-tonne market. *Jonathan Watt*

Working at altitude in the Chilean or Peruvian Andes places additional stresses on personnel and machines. The conditions required the engine of this Komatsu 830E to be fitted with larger turbochargers to maintain combustion efficiency and extra cooling to compensate for the thinner air.

harder to recruit sufficient numbers of skilled operators to the industry. With many large operations in remote locations, perched high in the Chilean or Peruvian Andes or in fly-in/fly-out sites in Canada for example, mining firms face a tough recruitment job. Some large South American copper mines can be at altitudes of up to 15,420 feet/4,700 meters and altitude sickness is a very real problem, so the prospect of operating a truck all year round in these conditions becomes a genuine challenge. The winter cold of Canadian mining operations poses another barrier to finding sufficient truck operators, and this could become a problem in other mining territories such as Siberia or Mongolia in future years. And when asked to justify the not-insignificant development cost of Caterpillar's 797 truck a few years ago, then-CEO Glen Barton replied, "I can answer that in two words; tar sands," a reference to the oil to be derived from tar sands in Canada's Athabasca tar sands region.

Whether the ultra-class trucks offer a true benefit in terms of cost/ton is open to debate. One of the main advantages of these bigger machines is undoubtedly that they allow mining firms to reduce the numbers of truck drivers they require to work at large operations in remote locations. Some mining industry experts maintain that the 240-U.S.-ton/216-tonne-sized trucks provide a better economic solution, especially since these machines are now benefiting from some of the advances developed initially for the ultra haulers. Both Unit Rig's MT4400 and Komatsu's 830E trucks are now available with more-sophisticated AC drives from GE, while Cat's trusty 793 mechanical-drive truck has been upgraded once more. Many mines still prefer to rely on this size class, as the long-term running costs are well understood, making things easier for the accountants who oversee the economic performance of mining operations.

All the same, the technological development of mining trucks continues, though it remains to be seen when or if even larger mine trucks will be built. There has been talk of machines with payloads of 500, 800, or even 1,000 U.S.

The scale of these rigid trucks may vary considerably, as do the detail design features from these different manufacturers, Liebherr and Terex, but similarities can be seen in terms of horsecollar design and general chassis layout.

Large mining operations require large fleets of large machines, with Barrick Gold using a fleet of Komatsu 930Es at this southwestern U.S. operation. *Kyran Casteel*

tons. It is debatable whether there are sufficient numbers of large mining operations to make all the research and development costs worthwhile to the manufacturers. While the tar sands operations of Canada might require bigger haulers, these firms would be unlikely to want to help fund the development of such machines. The manufacturers would have to see sufficient sales potential for bigger trucks before committing themselves fully to the very costly development process. The engineering involved would be substantial, as larger mine trucks would also have to overcome current capacity barriers set by available tires, drives, and engines. Perhaps twinned tires and all-wheel drives could be used once more, as on the BelAZ 7550 and Euclid R210. There is also the chance that Liebherr's innovative TI272, with its radical chassis design and low unladen weight, could point the way toward larger machines.

But this would still leave the problem of finding an engine with more power than the current king-of-the-heap, Detroit Diesel's 20V4000, which delivers 3,650 horsepower/2,721 kilowatts (just beating the Cat 3524B and Cummins QSK78 by around 100 horsepower/75 kilowatts). And as shown by Euclid's R210, gas turbines aren't a practical solution for an off-highway truck, while twin engines increase complexity, maintenance requirements, and running costs. Until such time as other power sources like fuel cells become a practical option for large mining machines (and it is impossible to determine when, or if, this will ever be feasible), diesel engines remain the best available technology.

Looking at the current ultra trucks, these machines all owe their existence as production machines to technological advances in the key areas of electric drives, tires, and diesel engines. The AC drives from GE, General Atomics, and Siemens (only Cat uses a mechanical drive) offer far higher outputs than the old DC systems, which had performance limitations. And AC drives also offer better acceleration from rest, better speed control, and more effective retardation. On top of that, AC drives are far less time-intensive to maintain than DC types, as they are

Continued on page 46

Next page: As one of these Komatsu 930E trucks backs up to the cable shovel for loading, another is already standing by to receive its load of ore. *Kyran Casteel*

The Grootegeluk Mine in South Africa has pioneered the use of AC-drive trucks on an overhead trolley line with its fleet of Hitachi EH4500s. *Jonathan Watt*

Continued from page 42

brushless (though bearing wear can be a problem with AC drives). However, with LeTourneau's introduction of switched reluctance motors on its wheel loaders, it remains to be seen whether this potentially even-more-advanced drive technology will cross over to the truck sector. Similarly, Bridgestone and Michelin's new generation of low-profile tires with 63-inch/1.6-meter rim sizes, as well as Goodyear's novel two-piece tires, allow bigger payloads. The evolution of large earthmoving equipment tires represents another substantial technological development, so much so it deserves full explanation in its own right.

It's important to note how much truck payload gains have relied on the technological development of engines, as the Caterpillar 3524B, Cummins QSK78, and Detroit Diesel 20V4000 all offer far higher outputs than any high-speed diesels built before. Previous large trucks like the Terex Titan, the V-Con, or BelAZ's 7550 (as well as the earlier LectraHaul M-200 and WABCO 3200/3200B) relied on heavy, low-speed locomotive engines. While these engines

offered sufficient power and were reliable, their rev range was limited, which restricted performance. Worse still, the heavy engine blocks (useful in a locomotive to maximize traction), increased the unladen weight of Terex's 33-19, BelAZ's 7550, or the V-Con, compromised their payload, and further added to an already high fuel consumption. Both the Terex Titan and BelAZ 7550 operated over several years, but neither model went into volume production, and none of the locomotive-engined trucks, including the earlier LectraHaul M-200 and 200B, can be considered truly successful.

Komatsu's 930E was the first machine with a payload greater than 240 U.S. tons/216 tonnes to achieve volume production, and by this measure can be regarded as the world's first truly successful ultra truck (based on the principle that badly flawed products don't tend to sell well). Even by 2001, total sales of Cat's 797, Komatsu's 930E, Liebherr's T282, and Unit Rig's MT5500 had already topped 300, and the market for machines in this class (now including Hitachi's EH5000 and Komatsu's new, larger machine, still in development at the time of writing) has continued to grow since that time.

The fleet of T282s bought for the Mount Arthur Coal operation in New South Wales, Australia, was fitted with special sound-suppression kits to minimize working noise generated at the site. *Liebherr collection*

Corporate changes have also had a notable effect on the dump truck market in recent years. During the 1990s, LeTourneau withdrew gradually from making trucks, and its mining equipment division now concentrates on its extremely successful large wheel loaders. Komatsu bought out Dresser in 1997, taking full control of the Haulpak range (Komatsu had built trucks with payloads up to 150 U.S. tons/135 tonnes in its Japanese factory). Terex, which since 1992 had supplied trucks with payloads up to 100 U.S. tons/91 tonnes to O&K to replace O&K's old Faun trucks, then bought out the O&K mine-shovel line at the end of 1997. These smaller Terex trucks are descended from much

earlier Euclid designs, as Terex's U.K. facility was originally built by Euclid. Hitachi, which had operated a joint venture with Volvo over the Euclid truck range since 1992, has since gone the whole way and bought the firm outright at the end of the 1990s, more or less dropping the Euclid name. Remembering Liebherr's acquisition of Wiseda, it is worth noting that of the big truck builders today, only Caterpillar has developed its entire truck line using purely in-house technology, without buying another firm.

These days, ownership of the big truck manufacturers has been concentrated in the hands of just six firms: BelAZ, Caterpillar, Hitachi, Komatsu, Liebherr, and

Liebherr's T282 was tested extensively, focusing on details such as the drive controls. Then the truck was developed further into the T282B, which offers an increased capacity with a 400-U.S.-ton/360-tonne payload. *Liebherr collection*

Terex. But it's worth remembering, too, that Italian firm Perlini offers a modern, five-model range that includes machines up to the top-of-the-line DP905, with a 105-U.S.-ton/95-tonne payload, allowing it to compete with Cat's popular 777, Hitachi's EH1600/EH1700, Komatsu's 785, and Terex's TR100. Similarly, the little Kansas firm Rimpull still makes three truck models with payloads of 85–150 U.S. tons/77–135 tonnes, and tractor/trailers for coal with 160–200-U.S.-ton/144–180-tonne capacities, though the firm concentrates on rebuild work. Also in the United States,

the Kress unitized coal haulers continue to be offered. And Randon in Brazil makes a line of small rigids that evolved from the Kockums designs, even though the Swedish manufacturer has long since disappeared (it became part-owned by Volvo and Euclid, with the small rigid models then being incorporated into the Hitachi lineup).

What the future holds for the mine-truck market is unclear, but it is certain that these huge machines will continue to evolve and improve. Whether they will grow significantly in payload, however, remains to be seen.

In the UK's smaller coal mining operations, 100-U.S.-ton/91-tonne trucks like this Terex TR100 are used widely for hauling overburden, with the loading operations carried out by 277-U.S.-ton/250-tonne-class mining shovels or excavators.

While Caterpillar's large mining trucks receive much attention due to their huge size, it is worth remembering that the company's small quarry trucks are still the bread and butter of the firm's rigid truck line.

Chapter 2
DIFFERENT STROKES
RADICAL RIGID TRUCK DESIGN

While other major manufacturers have followed tried-and-tested principles to design their large mine trucks, only Liebherr has attempted to push the boundaries by developing a machine along very different lines. True, Caterpillar's 797/797B uses a mechanical drivetrain to transmit power to the back wheels, unlike its rivals which use electric wheel motors. But the 797 and 797B are in effect scaled-up versions of the firm's well-proven mechanical drive range. Although different from machines from Hitachi, Komatsu, Liebherr, or Unit Rig, the 797 and 797B do not represent a radical departure from Caterpillar's own established engineering practice. By

Seen from the front, the TI272 does not reveal its innovative design, and the cab location, engine mounting, and double wishbone front suspension are all of a similar configuration to the firm's other trucks. *Liebherr collection*

comparison, Liebherr's TI272 is a large mine truck that stands out from the crowd.

Convention has seen the major manufacturers roll out trucks built along broadly similar lines, with an engine at the front, two axles, twinned tires at the rear fitted to a rigid axle, and a heavy-duty, rigid chassis providing structural strength. Even Cat's mechanical-drive 797 and 797B follow this pattern. But Liebherr's TI272 is different, with a much lighter-duty chassis and much of the rigidity instead provided by the dump body for an overall saving in unladen weight. In concept, this is not so far from the way many modern motorcycles and racing cars use the engine as a stressed member, in order to do away with part of the chassis and reduce overall weight, as this brings obvious benefits for speed and handling capabilities. However, to make its lightweight chassis work, the TI272 also requires an unusual rear drive, with the two sets of twinned tires being driven independently of each other.

The origins of the TI272 are unusual, too, as they lie originally with the Australian mining company BHP (later merged with British firm Billiton to form BHP Billiton, becoming one of the top three mining companies in the world). It is rare indeed for a mining company to have pioneered the development of a new mine truck, as it is more common for manufacturers to enlist the help of mining firms during new model development. BHP, however, bucked this trend, and during the 1980s its in-house research team began looking at ways to cut a chunk out of haulage costs and boost mine operating effectiveness, and this included coming up with ideas for ways to make the trucks more efficient. A key point came when the team identified that improving the payload-to-machine-weight ratio could allow firms to maintain payload capacity, while cutting fuel and tire costs. Short of utilizing exotic and costly lightweight aircraft-grade alloys based on aluminum, magnesium, or even titanium in place of steel, though, the only way to deliver this was to take a fresh look at the mine truck.

Clearly, the design of a truck was crucial, and this quickly became a focal point. Improving conventional payload-to-weight ratios, mostly around the 1.3:1 to 1.4:1 band, to 1.75:1 or higher, could provide substantial cost reductions. By the late 1980s, BHP's engineers had come up with the basic design for a haul truck. However, BHP Research was well aware that while it had plenty of

The sloping side bolsters play a major role in stiffening the whole of the TI272's dump-body structure, so that it can provide the strength required for the entire truck. *Liebherr collection*

experience with digging minerals out of the ground, it would require a manufacturer to actually develop a truck. The search for a suitable partner began in the early 1990s. And as BHP had been buying mine trucks from Wiseda, which pioneered the 240-U.S.-ton/216-tonne class with its KL-2450 in the early 1980s, it was entirely logical that the Kansas-based firm would be chosen to help.

The BHP team showed its initial design sketches to Wiseda's engineers, and it was clear from the outset that these had considerable potential. Wiseda accepted the challenge, and, now called the Innovative Large Mining Truck project (ILMT), the development work gathered apace. A feasibility study helped fine-tune the original design, with a number of improvements to the chassis configuration suggested by Wiseda's engineers. The joint team from BHP

and Wiseda also reckoned that to keep costs in trim, it would make sense to utilize as many components as possible from the existing and well-proven KL-2450 truck.

With Wiseda's engineers now working on the project, a strong design influence came to bear, and as the front end of the ILMT began to take shape, the initial prototype began to feature a similar outline to the KL-2450. The machine used the same 2,470-horsepower/1,840-kilowatt MTU 16V396 engine, General Electric GTA-26 generator, double wishbone suspension, power module, and a broadly similar subframe. But the back end of the machine was radically different, with an all-new approach to the design and layout of the frame, dump body, rear suspension, and electric drive.

One of the key points of the ILMT was its rear-suspension and drive configuration. The twin drives were entirely

The TI272 represents a radical departure from established design convention, and its layout may well provide a solution for larger payloads, as well as ways to reduce haulage costs for the smaller capacities of existing truck classes. *Liebherr collection*

independent, both featuring a DC motor, a differential, and reduction gearing. The motors selected were well-proven GE-787 FS6 units, installed in special housings built by Australian firm Birrana Engineering, which also made the reduction gears. These cylindrical housings were mounted longitudinally and in parallel with the frame rails, rather than at right angles as in a conventional electric-drive truck. The power was then transferred from the motors to the rear wheels by separate differentials, which for the prototype ILMT were components more commonly seen in Caterpillar's 994 wheel loader. The front portion of each of these assemblies was hitched mid-way along the frame by pivot joints. Suspension points for the drive assemblies

were located on the main frame at the same spot as the body pivot points. This novel rear-drive/suspension system was a radical departure, as it allowed the twin rear axles to rotate separately. Several advantages were identified as a result of the rotating twinned axles, such as the fact that the truck would be less vulnerable to excessive tire wear caused by different diameters (itself a function of wear) or varying tire pressures. Put simply, the rotation offered by the separate differentials would take up or offset any variations in tire diameter arising from tire wear or differing pressures. This had the effect of spreading the load more equally and reducing the risk of overloading any individual tires or causing further wear. The even weight distribution also allowed the ILMT to be matched more accurately to the required tires than were conventional machines, as the engineers could count on the machine exerting specific loads at the rear axle in correlation to the payload carried.

Some additional chassis stiffness was required, so an underbody crossmember was fitted to link the motor pivot points, though the rear of the frame broke with tradition by being open-ended without a crossmember (and also by being wider than usual). Meanwhile, having the motor assembly mountings in the same spot as the body pivot points ensured that any stresses generated as the truck drove over an uneven surface would be transferred directly to the dump body structure rather than to the frame itself.

Because the two drive assemblies were intended to move independently of each other, the BHP and Wiseda engineers figured that when it came to crossing uneven ground, the ILMT would offer better performance than a conventional truck with a solid/live axle. In effect, the ILMT's rear-drive configuration also offered the benefit of truly independent rear suspension. With this layout, the ILMT's tires would be able to cope with undulations across the axle, providing better traction as the tires would not lift from the ground (unless extremely poor conditions were encountered). Moreover, the ILMT's rear-drive layout would also minimize tire scrubbing in turns and reduce the risk of traction loss in the wet, a benefit directly attributable to the separate differentials. Rather than the twinned tires on either side of the truck acting together through a central differential as on a conventional machine, the ILMT's rear tires could all follow their own individual track, providing benefits to tire life and traction.

The design and location of the dump body was the other crucial factor in the ILMT's overall concept, as it provided a considerable portion of the structural rigidity required by the whole machine. The idea was that the weight of the body would sit more or less directly onto the suspension, reducing stresses exerted on the frame. The body was supported by the two pivots at the rear, with the lift cylinders at the front then mounted directly behind the horsecollar. According to the engineers, the tire struts were pinned to the dump body with a split shackle arrangement, allowing vertical and side loads to be transferred down from the body and through the suspension into the ground. With this layout, loads from the suspension could also be transferred into the dump body, without the need for a rear chassis crossmember to provide additional chassis stiffness. And it was this last feature that delivered the team's aim of providing

a major weight saving for the chassis and for the truck as a whole. However, as the dump body pivot points were roughly three times wider than normal, this had another benefit too. It allowed a more stable load distribution, reducing the problems often seen on conventional trucks that can sometimes "wallow" on a poorly constructed or maintained haul road. In addition, the design also spread the payload, so that the bending stresses exerted on the frame would be reduced.

To make all this work, both the body design and hoist system had to be different from anything yet built. Two multistage hoist cylinders were fitted just above the front suspension units, providing a direct path into the dump body for any stresses generated from uneven terrain that weren't soaked up by the double wishbone layout. These cylinders had the additional job of locating the body when it was carrying a load and ensuring there could be no sideways movement. Meanwhile, the body's structural role dictated that it had to be made from special grades of steel, with much stiffer floor, canopy, and front plate than convention dictated. In addition, a single bolster was fitted on each side that sloped up from the rear dump pivot to the side of the front canopy.

Although in scale the prototype truck was similar to the 240-U.S.-ton/216-tonne-class machines, its vital statistics revealed the payload advantage. Gross vehicle weight was just under 388 U.S. tons/350 tonnes, with an intended weight distribution of 130 U.S. tons/116 tonnes at the front and 258 U.S. tons/232 tonnes at the rear. By comparison, gross machine weight for one of the conventional 240-U.S.-ton/216-tonne-payload trucks of the time would have been around 426 U.S. tons/384 tonnes or so. And bear in mind that even in its original form, the ILMT was offering a payload of 249 U.S. tons/225 tonnes and had a body capacity of 162 cubic yards/127 cubic meters, a notable gain over more traditional designs. Although the engineering team had not quite managed to reach its original target payload-to-weight ratio, the 1.72:1 figure the ILMT offered in reality still represented a huge gain over the conventional truck models.

It was during the development of the ILMT that Liebherr made its move to acquire the Wiseda business in mid-1995. Seeing the potential for this machine and the close links that had been forged with BHP, Liebherr continued the project, though ILMT now stood for Innovative Liebherr Mining Truck. The research-and-development program continued, and with the first prototype completed,

Next page: Because each set of the TI272's twinned wheels is free to rotate about the end of its suspension unit, the tires are able to follow undulations in the ground, equalizing load and reducing wear. *Liebherr collection*

another three units were built. Once testing of the initial prototype got underway at Central Queensland Coal Associates' Saraji mine in Queensland, Australia (then operated by BHP), and the machine began to clock up hours in the dirt, various factors became apparent and design tweaks were made. The differential bearings needed some attention, as the lubrication in the original layout was not sufficient, so the engineering team redesigned this area. In addition, running the truck on very uneven terrain did cause a wheel to lift off the ground, suggesting that a limited-slip differential system might be required to prevent traction loss in poor operating conditions.

However, these were the sort of teething problems expected of a new machine, particularly one that represented such a radical departure from conventional design. An evaluation of the ILMT prototype's running costs suggested savings in the order of 14 to 18 percent, not bad for a machine that featured so many new ideas. The ILMT's performance in the dirt also showed some benefits over conventional machines. And a key point was that the novel oscillating rear-drive/suspension assembly had shown its ability to improve handling in the wet and offer better weight distribution than conventional rigid axles. Drivers testing the first prototype truck commented favorably with regard to the gains in steering and ride characteristics the machine offered, as well as the good tipping/load-dumping performance and its improved rear visibility. This last feature gave a noted advantage when reversing towards the loading equipment or to the dump areas and provided an unexpected safety gain.

However, development of this new concept truck wasn't all as straightforward as Liebherr would have liked. As the trials progressed, fatigue problems were noted in some of the frame sections of all four prototypes. As a result, Liebherr opted to redesign the chassis, with the added benefit of increasing the truck's load capacity. To evaluate the structural stresses fully and to pinpoint the trouble spots, Liebherr placed strain gauges on the prototypes so that the machines could be tested under working conditions. As expected, these tests highlighted the radical nature of the chassis, which performed in a different manner than conventional machines. Liebherr then hired a specialist from a new firm, Mechanical Simulation International, to develop a computer model of the chassis to evaluate its performance. The specialist, Ford Cook, utilized a technique called multibody dynamic simulation, running on software from Belgian firm LMS International, and his results backed up the findings of the on-site load tests. The computer-based model brought additional information too, so Liebherr's team decided to buy the LMS DADS mechanical system simulation software from LMS International and then started refining it.

The on-site tests and subsequent computer analysis had given valuable information as to how Liebherr should proceed with the project. With experience, the Liebherr team was able to improve the model so that it contained over 30 different structures, representing the major moving parts as well as a number of the welded components or bolted assemblies. Using proven Pro-Engineer software to make production and finite element models allowed the team to establish inertia properties and formed the basis for graphics used subsequently for animations. Shell and simplified beam models of the frame were modelled on the computer, and the engineers first ensured that these matched each other, then used the beam model in its multi-body analysis. The team modeled the truck's dump body as a rigid structure joined to other parts by bushings, with its stiffness established by finite element analysis to evaluate the flexibility. Liebherr utilized joint elements to connect these bodies and model components, with bushing elements simulating rubber pads and translational damper actuators to model the damping effects of struts and hydraulic cylinders. Meanwhile, expression force elements were employed to simulate the torques generated by brakes or drive motors, as well as the forces from steering and hoist cylinders, and even to model contacts between the hoist cylinders and guides. Similarly, contact elements modeled the axle rotation stops that limit pivot movement, with curve elements being used to specify electric motors, hydraulic pumps, suspension struts, and tires. The computer model became so detailed that even the low-pressure 50/80 R57 radial tires were modeled using information supplied by Michelin.

By using the computer model Cook had developed, the engineering team was able to investigate different configurations for the truck and change operating conditions to evaluate changes to the design of the machine. The areas of the prototype that had suffered fatigue problems were tackled using the computer model to simulate forces and determine loads for finite element analysis. The model could simulate complete haul cycles, so the engineers could identify the various stresses generated as the truck carried out different tasks, such as loading, hauling, backing up to the dump site, tipping, and even acceleration and deceleration. As Liebherr's engineers became more used to using the program, they were able to simulate lane changing or steady cornering and more extreme conditions such as full power or retardation, running over potholes or fallen rock, and explosive tire failures.

Using this technology allowed the Liebherr engineers to redesign the frame and a number of other structural components, without adding greatly to the overall weight of the truck. Switching to castings instead of using fabricated

Several TI272s were put to work at mines around the world as part of the development process to analyze the performance of components, and this resulted in changes to some components. *Liebherr collection*

components was one of the moves, while selecting larger tires, a more powerful engine, and one of the then-new Siemens AC drives would boost all-round performance. In addition, the Caterpillar 994 differentials used at first were replaced with purpose-built units from LNS. Using all these design improvements allowed Liebherr to boost the ILMT's payload to 300 U.S. tons/270 tonnes initially, with a target figure of 320 U.S. tons/290 tonnes once the improved model had been tested thoroughly.

Several design changes were made during the evolution of the ILMT into the TI272, following the extensive trials. The body design for the TI272 retained many of the features of the prototype ILMT units, while now offering a heaped capacity of 209 cubic yards/164 cubic meters. The side ribs of the body were sloped slightly, as this was the

most effective way to provide the structural stiffness required. And as the body performed the function of providing stiffness to the whole truck, the machine was fitted with interlocks preventing it from being driven with the body in the raised position. The hoist cylinders were modified slightly, as was the software running the system, and with these changes, the TI272 achieved a body-raise/dump time of 20 seconds, with a float time of 15 seconds and a 12-second lower time.

The engine was changed to the newer and more powerful MTU/Detroit Diesel 16V4000 unit rated at 2,700 horsepower/2,013 kilowatts, which offered several benefits over the older diesel in terms of response, reliability, and fuel consumption. With this engine, the TI272 was good for a top speed of 43 miles per hour/68 kilometers per hour, and testing soon showed the newer design offered far better retardation due to the AC technology from Siemens. Like the ILMT, though, the TI272's reduction gears were still located in the wheels, so each truck had four of these assemblies in all. The TI272 was designed for use with either 44/80R57 or 46/90R57 tires as standard (depending on the application), and as mentioned earlier, the Liebherr engineers knew the design of the rear suspension would offer effective load distribution. The benefit to tire life arising from this was another advantage in the TI272's favor due to its ability to keep stresses within rated loads, as well as to reduce tire scrubbing because of the twinned differentials.

Some of the original aims, such as that of reducing fuel consumption, were further aided by the switch to the newer engine and more efficient AC drives. This more than made up for the slight penalty in mechanical efficiency incurred by driving the rear wheels through the separate differentials, in addition to the reduction gears in the wheel assemblies. According to Siemens, the AC drives provided an efficiency saving of 7 or 8 percent over the earlier DC units, and Liebherr reckoned the TI272 could deliver fuel savings of 10 to 15 percent in comparison with other trucks with the same payload. The firm also estimated fuel savings of $3 to $6 per pound per year for each truck from the better fuel economy alone.

Other modifications and improvements for the TI272 in comparison with the ILMT prototypes included new software and changes to various hydraulic systems. Once all the updates were complete, empty weight for the TI272 was around 155 U.S. tons/140 tonnes, which compared well with the 168.5 U.S. tons/152 tonnes for Liebherr's conventional T262, aimed at the 240-U.S.-ton/216-tonne-capacity class.

One of the first TI272s went to the Thabazimbi iron ore operation in South Africa, and this was for a while the largest truck in Africa, as well as one of the first ultra trucks on the continent. Other TI272s went for testing at Lee Ranch in Wyoming and at Mount Owen in New South Wales, Australia. The machine at Thabazimbi was used for hauling both ore and overburden at the Donkerpoort West pit, an unusual operation in that the trucks haul full loads downhill to the tip and return empty.

One site-specific point regarding AC-drive trucks of all makes is that these offer better speed control than older DC systems, so the superior retardation characteristics of the new Siemens drives certainly came in useful. Trucks fitted with AC drives also show better startup characteristics and acceleration from rest than those with conventional DC systems, so it was no surprise that the TI272 scored well in this regard too.

For the moment, the future for the TI272 is unclear. But it is fair to say that with the TI272, Liebherr has gone further than any other manufacturer so far in terms of real engineering effort and investment to move away from established truck design concepts. While curiosities such as Euclid's gas turbine–powered R210 or the V-Con truck reached prototype stage in the 1970s, these projects were quickly shown to be impractical. The TI272 may yet show itself to represent the way forward for the mine truck. Liebherr did consider mating the engine and drives from the T282, as well as 63-inch/1.6-meter-rim-size tires from Bridgestone or Michelin to a larger version of the TI272's chassis layout. This could provide a truck with a payload in excess of 443 U.S. tons/400 tonnes, although it would take some redesigning to squeeze the wider R63 tires into the twinned rear-drive system, and it would require a wider track as well as possibly reducing the degree of oscillation. Only time will tell how mine trucks will develop in years to come, but one thing is certain: Liebherr's TI272 has been a major design milestone along the way.

Chapter 3
ROBOT TRUCKS
MINING WITH PERSONAL COMPUTERS

It was in September 1996 that Caterpillar made history, unveiling to an assembled crowd of mining industry professionals and journalists a radical new technology the firm had been working on in secret for some time. As the spectators sat in the hot Arizona sun, a 777C mine truck drew to a halt in the dry and dusty demonstration area in front of them at Caterpillar's Tinaja Hills test facility. The operator first shut down the engine, then opened the door, climbed down the ladder, and walked away from the parked truck. Moments later, the engine fired up and there was a puff of smoke from its exhaust, as the world's first demonstration of a robot mine truck got underway.

The 777 then drove around the demonstration area as its computerized operator put it through its paces. The

truck drove toward a loading area and, together with another computer-controlled 777, had its dump body filled conventionally by a manually controlled wheel loader. This was no trick either. The 777 truck was under computer control, and there really wasn't anyone in its cab.

As the demonstration continued, one of the Caterpillar personnel walked nonchalantly in front of the fully laden 777 as it roared along its short section of haul road at up to 40 miles per hour/64 kilometers per hour in the demonstration area. Weighing over 172 U.S. tons/155 tonnes, the truck stopped abruptly, pitching forward on its front suspension as its brakes brought the heavily laden machine to a halt in the minimum distance possible. Sitting among the audience, it was impossible to tell whether the

Robot trucks have yet to make their mark in surface mining, but computer-controlled loaders are already proving their worth at underground mining applications in Australia, Chile, Sweden, and South Africa.

The first operation running a fleet of robot loaders in a true production environment was LKAB's Kiruna iron ore mine in northern Sweden. The machines started work in the 1990s, although this system uses an early-generation technology.

demonstrator had been sweating unduly as he'd placed himself in the path of a fully laden truck that didn't have anyone in its cab and had been traveling at full speed.

The ongoing announcement over the loudspeaker told everything as it happened. The truck was equipped with a forward-scanning radar system mounted on its front bumper that could detect obstacles in its path and either instruct the machine to drive around the obstruction if there was sufficient room or put the brakes on—hard.

This part of the demonstration over, the machine then turned, found a spot to dump its load, and trundled off to join the other robot truck, which was being loaded up by a conventionally operated Caterpillar wheel loader. The two haulers then followed a preset path set by the demonstrator who was sitting behind the wheel of a Chevrolet Blazer, controlling the operations using a PC. The announcer explained that the controller was going to instruct the machines to change direction to simulate avoiding an obstacle on the haul road, which the trucks duly did. Further

demonstration followed as the trucks drove around, dumped their loads, and returned to the waiting wheel loader to be filled with more rock and dirt. At the end of this demonstration, one of the 777s drew to a halt in front of the audience, which was invited to give it a quick look over. And sure enough, there wasn't anyone in the cab.

The truck was fitted with an impressive antenna array, with the small radar system just above the front bumper for forward object detection, a small cone-shaped GPS unit above the cab, and a multipronged communications system above the engine. The GPS unit told the truck where it was at any one time, while the communications array had the job of shuttling all the position and performance data, as well as commands, back and forth to the onboard computer that drove the truck.

This demonstration was the culmination of several years of testing, first in lab simulations and then in a working quarry site in Alabama. After lunch, the audience at Tinaja Hills was told somewhat confidently that it would take five years or so but that by the new millennium, robot mine trucks would begin to be commercially available to the mining industry. Clearly, that prediction was somewhat premature. While robot trucks have certainly been tested over long periods in true mining applications, the industry has yet to begin ordering such technology en masse.

The firm was making a serious point with the robot trucks, though perhaps Cat's faith in its innovative new technology was premature. The system was still expensive and its advanced technology untried. But it seems likely that the slump in the mining industry that followed the demonstration of the robot trucks was a bigger factor in delaying the implementation of this radical system than doubts over the actual quality of the technology. When the jump in the market for mined materials came, the industry was hard-pressed to respond because of the steep rise in demand, and the industry was not in a position to take a gamble on untried technology. Once again, the robot truck's implementation had been held back primarily by economic, rather than technical, factors.

The mining industry is a conservative one. It is entirely understandable that no firm wants to be the first to try a radical new technology that is possibly going to be full of bugs (however minor) that will interrupt production and have a serious impact on running costs and productivity. When it comes to testing larger shovels or bigger trucks with new drivelines, the larger mining companies can just about countenance operating a new machine, especially when the manufacturer offers performance guarantees and backup equipment. But the robot truck concept was a step beyond this. The robot trucks would not operate individually, but rather came as a system, and the mining industry was understandably wary.

It was no great surprise, then, when Caterpillar's archrival Komatsu revealed soon after that it, too, had been working on robot trucks, having first tested the machines at a quarry in Japan. Like the Caterpillar trucks, the Komatsu machines were equipped with GPS equipment to identify position at all times. A radar device fitted to the front bumper/fender had the job of identifying obstructions,

Conventional industrial computing hardware is used to run both the Sandvik Tamrock Automine and Caterpillar Minegem robot underground loader systems.

Sandvik Tamrock developed its computerized Automine system at its test mine facility, located next to its factory at Tampere in Finland.

and, as with the Caterpillar 777s first demonstrated at Tinaja Hills, this system would either make the machine drive around what was in its path or put the brakes on.

The computer controlling both the Caterpillar and Komatsu trucks was based on standard-though-powerful PC hardware. The software used by Komatsu trucks was based around the proven dispatch package developed by Komatsu's software subsidiary Modular Mining. Following its announcement that its robot trucks existed and the description of the basic system specification, Komatsu also revealed that a small fleet of these machines was operating at a metal mine in Western Australia. And, unlike the Caterpillar system, these machines were running alongside conventionally operated trucks on the same haul roads. Though there were the inevitable software glitches at first, the results were extremely promising. Benefits soon became apparent, as the computers were easier on the trucks than human operators, reducing maintenance needs. And, as one of Modular Mining's technical personnel

said at the time, "They follow each other's wheel tracks as if they're running on rails."

While Caterpillar then decided the time was not yet right for its robot trucks to become a commercial proposition and put its project on hold, Komatsu persisted with its research, first by testing machines for some years in the United States and then in Chile. Both firms agreed on the potential of this technology. There is a need for robot equipment able to work continuously with minimal supervision, and this is increasing as health and safety issues become ever-more-tightly regulated. Many of the world's big new mines are in remote areas that are difficult to access. The large copper mines of Chile and Peru can be at altitudes of up to 15,420 feet/4,700 meters in the Andes, and running an operation at such a height poses major hazards to health and safety. Winter conditions at these mines can be brutal, with biting cold, high winds, blizzards, and the very real risk of avalanches. And even in midsummer, the physical problems imposed on the human

Chilean copper producer Codelco is using a fleet of robot loaders developed initially by Sandvik Tamrock at its Finnish test facility for the huge El Teniente mine for production in two separate areas.

frame are ever present. At such altitudes, people suffer badly. The thin air means that oxygen levels are low, and even a small effort that would be easily accomplished at lower altitudes becomes a major physical chore. While a fit and healthy person can remain conscious at altitudes of up to 18,000 feet/5,500 meters or so, trying to carry out a job of work over a full working shift at such a height is another thing altogether. For example, something as normal as running up a short flight of stairs at such an altitude can cause a fit of dizziness and even trigger a blackout. For this reason, it is not unrealistic that mining firms should fit oxygen equipment or even pressurized cabs to machines being used at the world's highest operations.

But the additional operating costs of such remote mines are by no means limited to fitting breathing equipment in machines. Weather conditions can make flying in crews risky, while access roads can be tortuous and potentially lethal in winter, with a high risk of avalanches, rock falls, treacherous curves, and steep gradients all conspiring to make traveling to and from the mine difficult and dangerous.

The Chilean and Peruvian copper mines are not alone in finding it hard to recruit staff. In Canada, the fast-growing tar sands operations provide another good market for robot truck technology. Though these operations are not at extremes of altitude, they are in remote locations with extremely arduous winter conditions. Meanwhile, there are very different physical challenges experienced at mines in Western Australia and Chile's Atacama Desert. Home to some of the world's most cost-efficient, large iron ore and gold mines, Western Australia's daylight temperatures are among the hottest on Earth. Similar high temperatures are also seen at the large copper mines in the Atacama Desert, which is the driest place on the planet. Finding sufficient water for a process plant is bad enough without having to ensure there is enough potable water for the personnel to avoid dehydration.

Many mining firms now report finding it harder and harder to recruit trained machine operators. And the housing facilities required by a large mine may resemble a small town, a colossal expense when working in a remote location. Adding together the cost of transporting skilled personnel to these remote sites to operate equipment, housing them with a reasonable degree of comfort, and paying them enough to stay on the job, it is understandable that robot trucks offer an interesting economic alternative. Anything mining firms can do to reduce these costs could have potential financial benefits. Robot trucks may be expensive to buy, but they do not have to be fed and watered and are not likely to grumble about poor living facilities or the need for a pay raise.

Surprising as it may seem, robot mining machines have already been running for some years in production applications too. Experimental systems were tested in the 1990s, but when the first true production robot-operated machines began operating, it was no real surprise that this was in an underground mining environment, rather than at a surface mine. Swedish iron ore producer LKAB pushed the boundaries of technology as part of its KUJ 2000 project, when setting up a new mine level at its Kiruna mine in the north of the country. This system allowed one human operator to supervise the running of three underground loaders (called LHDs, or load haul dumps) at a time. The machines were able to negotiate the tunnels and carry out the bucket dumping part of the working cycle themselves under computer control. The human operator sits in a control room in a different part of the mine and is only required to fill the bucket at the loading point, a task that is difficult to automate due to the widely differing size and weight characteristics of blasted rock. Swedish-owned Sandvik Tamrock supplied a fleet of its giant 28-U.S.-ton/25-tonne-payload 2500E LHD models to LKAB, and this system has now been operating successfully for some years. With water in the tires for traction, these giant loaders weigh nearly 110 U.S. tons/100 tonnes apiece, and LKAB has a whole fleet of the machines running under computer control at Kiruna. Meanwhile in Australia, the North Parkes and Olympic Dam underground mines have also been running experimental Caterpillar Elphinstone LHDs, but in genuine production applications that have proven the technology.

But it was Chilean copper producer Codelco's vast El Teniente operation (the world's largest underground mine) that first put its money on the table to order a fleet of robot equipment, a deal made public in late 2003. Codelco, the world's largest copper producer, opted for the Sandvik Tamrock Automine system that had been tried extensively in the manufacturer's own test mine in Finland. The order was for two separate Automine systems to operate in different parts of El Teniente mine and run six Tamrock Toro LHDs simultaneously. Like the machines at LKAB's Kiruna mine, the LHDs navigate the tunnels and dump the buckets under computer control with an operator located elsewhere in the mine only needed to fill the bucket. In this manner, two operators can supervise the operation of all six LHDs simultaneously. However, the Automine package Codelco opted for is a more advanced system than the earlier-generation technology used by LKAB, which relies heavily on reflector equipment to allow the machines to identify their position. Automine, and Caterpillar's rival Minegem system, uses scanning lasers mounted at the front and back of the LHDs to allow the machines to identify their location in the tunnel by cross-checking the data with a computerized map. Both of these systems can learn, too, and should the lasers identify new features of the tunnels, this information will be added to the computerized mine map.

Conventional industrial computers are used for the hardware to keep costs down, and it is the software running the system that holds the key to its performance. The software decides which part of the loading area the LHDs should be operating in and where they should go next. The machines are able to follow different routes and pick up and dump in different locations so as to maximize throughput or balance ore grade as it enters the crusher.

The results of using robot LHDs at Kiruna, North Parkes, Olympic Dam, and El Teniente have been impressive, and all of these mines report similar benefits. Under computer control, the machines are far less likely to hit the tunnel walls, which cuts a major chunk out of annual repair bills, and the LHDs can be run at full speed, increasing their productivity. The computers are also easier on the equipment, with gear changes made at optimum times, reduced wear and tear on tires because the computers balance power delivery and minimize tire slip, and so on. The computers do not get tired and make more mistakes towards the end of a shift, nor do they require coffee or cigarette breaks, for example. All in all, automated loading actually cuts maintenance costs for the LHD fleet, while maximizing productivity.

Other robot systems are now being used too, and some of these are more sophisticated still. The DeBeers Finsch underground diamond mine in South Africa bought a complete Automine package comprising automated LHDs and trucks. As at North Parkes, Olympic Dam, Kiruna, and El Teniente, human operators are required to fill the buckets. However, the LHDs drive by themselves and dump their bucket loads under computer guidance into the mine trucks, which are also robots.

There are good reasons why robot machines are beginning to be accepted in underground mining before they are in surface mining. In underground mining, there are far tougher restrictions on health and safety issues than in surface mining. Using robot machines enables mining firms like LKAB and Codelco to operate efficiently and productively, even in areas where conditions would not be suitable for manned equipment to run. Although LKAB and Codelco use their machines solely for production throughput, robot LHDs offer other potential benefits. For development work, robot LHDs could return to the face as soon as blasting was complete and without having to worry about blasting fumes that would be harmful to health, for instance.

The fact that the underground mining sector is beginning to accept robot machines at large, high-production mines points the way forward. This technology *does* work and the surface-mining industry will follow, as it stands to gain similar benefits.

RUBBER RINGS
TIRE TECHNOLOGY

It was the highly inventive R. G. LeTourneau who first pioneered the use of pneumatic tires on off-highway equipment, despite comments from his contemporaries that this would, in all likelihood, be impractical. True, dump trucks had been using solid and then pneumatic tires for some years, but when LeTourneau experimented with these on a towed scraper box in 1932, he achieved a quantum leap in earthmoving efficiency. Using pneumatic truck tires in place of steel wheels showed what LeTourneau had already suspected: major gains in performance resulting in substantially more dirt being moved per shift. The rubber tires increased productivity due

largely to the fact that they provided a cushion effect that reduced the shock loads on the towing vehicle and allowed the scraper bowl to more or less float over the bumps and take a much bigger bite out of the surface material. The cushioning effect of using tires instead of steel wheels minimized the stresses on the scraper and reduced wear and tear and equipment maintenance needs. While this wasn't rocket science and was a logical step, given the advantages already seen in the automotive sector by replacing solid tires with pneumatic ones, many had questioned whether the same rules would apply in the much tougher earthmoving environment. But as LeTourneau showed, pneumatic tires

Even in the early days of truck haulage in the 1920s, extensive testing was required in tough conditions to ensure tire performance and life would match the rigors of site use. *Michelin collection*

allowed far greater operating efficiencies than steel wheels in the scraper application.

However, there were still major setbacks, as the only tires available at that time were designed for road trucks, and LeTourneau found these gave poor service in off-highway applications. Punctures and other failures abounded, so LeTourneau voiced his criticisms of the tires he was using somewhat loudly, initially to little response. Eventually, though, he managed to persuade Firestone that the off-highway equipment market was sufficiently large that it would be worthwhile to offer products able to meet the rugged requirements of the job. Two years later, Firestone introduced the first purpose-developed earth-mover tires, and these found a ready market, primarily in the U.S. construction sector.

However, even these tires had their shortcomings due to the technological limitations of the period, restricting payload and wear life. It was French firm Michelin that made the next step, introducing tires that utilized steel cord instead of textiles to increase wear life, durability, and capacity. These tires were aimed initially at the rail market, at a new breed of railcar designed to run on pneumatic tires instead of conventional steel wheels in a bid to provide a smoother ride. (The Paris Metro underground railway still uses this approach, offering a ride quality that is unparalleled.) This was a crucial stage, because although steel belting had been tried in tires before, there had been technical problems. The manufacturers had not been able to achieve a reliable bond between the rubber and the steel. Until Michelin found a solution, the structure of the experimental steel-belted tires simply failed in testing, as the steel separated from the rubber after a short period of use. In the 1930s, Michelin got around the problem and managed to develop a method that provided a reliable bond between the steel and rubber, with the firm's first Metallic tires featuring this more durable belting. This major step was achieved by hot dipping the steel in brass prior to using it as belting, which allowed Michelin to increase the load capacity for truck tires substantially. Accounts differ as to whether these became available commercially in 1937 or 1939, but by the time World War II started, tires of belted steel were coming onto the market. As one of Michelin's major factories was based in the United Kingdom, the Allies had access to the technology. At the same time, though, German forces were also able to benefit when they invaded France, where

By 1950, tire manufacturers were able to offer products that could last the distance on haul trucks such as these 25-U.S.-ton/23-tonne-capacity Euclids. *Michelin collection*

Michelin had a long and close relationship with car manufacturer Citröen that predated its development of earthmover tires by many years. *Michelin collection*

Michelin was based, capturing valuable information on the steel-belting technique.

After the war had come to a close, Firestone, Goodyear, and Michelin all began competing in the off-highway equipment sector, and these three firms made progressive developments with tires aimed at this market, developing larger and more durable units that lasted longer and carried more. The improvement in tire technology came in parallel with the development of larger trucks with bigger payloads, which grew substantially from the small machines of the 1940s, fueled by a rapid period of industrial growth and high demand for minerals and aggregates. It was Michelin again that first introduced the radial tire, initially for the automotive sector and then, in 1959, introducing its first radial for the earthmoving equipment market.

Since that time, earthmover tires have continued to grow steadily in size to match the increase in the scale of the trucks and other machines being developed, with Firestone (later bought out by Japanese firm Bridgestone), Goodyear, and Michelin all making huge improvements in their products. By 1971, for instance, the largest rim sizes Michelin offered had diameters of 51 inches/1.295 meters, and this had grown to 57 inches/1.45 meters by 1973. Development continued so that by 1976, the largest radial tire Michelin had available weighed 4.74 U.S. tons/4.28 tonnes, with Firestone and Goodyear making parallel developments in their own product lines.

Tire technology had always been one of the limiting factors on machine design, and this is certainly true of the earthmoving equipment market, ever since R. G. LeTourneau first tried pneumatic tires on his scraper boxes. In the early 1990s, when Caterpillar introduced its 994 wheel loader, a tire was developed somewhat quickly that was based on an existing unit for the truck market. This new tire used the same tread pattern and sidewall design, with a

This Berliet T100 truck was built specially in the mid-1950s as an oil-supply vehicle for use in the desert and required a special 33-inch/0.83-meter-rim tire to cope with the extreme heat. The truck also shared many features with the firm's 111-U.S.-ton/100-tonne hauler. *Michelin collection*

spacer in the middle to give it extra width. However, in the dirt, the performance of this tire proved less than satisfactory due to the very different operating cycle of a wheel loader than a rigid dump truck, and this resulted in rapid wear. Seeing a need for more durable products, both Bridgestone Firestone and Michelin soon developed improved designs that were specially for the large wheel loader application. Michelin's original tire for the 994 may have been a slick that weighed 6.4 U.S. tons/5.8 tonnes and had to be fitted with chains for traction, but it allowed a huge improvement in wear life over the widened truck tires that had been used previously. Meanwhile, Bridgestone Firestone worked with LeTourneau to develop tires for the L-1800 wheel loader (and successive models such as the upgraded L-1850 and subsequent L-2350).

The different tire firms believed in different technologies, though, with Bridgestone Firestone and Goodyear relying primarily on bias-ply tires for the earthmoving market for many years, and Michelin steadily introducing radials to its lineup. By 1980, Michelin was offering radial tires for machines right across the earthmoving equipment sector, and seeing that some customers preferred this type, Bridgestone Firestone and Goodyear also developed their own radials, admitting these had some benefits in certain applications.

For the truck market, though, the availability of suitable tires had long been a key design issue. Truck manufacturers wanted to develop machines with bigger payloads, and while they understood the engineering requirements necessary in building larger chassis and so on, they were limited by the available tire technology. The Terex Titan of the early 1970s

The LeTourneau wheeled dozer broke technical barriers, but the nature of the duty cycle demanded that special tires had to be developed that could provide the traction required and that were also extremely durable. *Michelin collection*

represented a quantum leap in terms of payload, and it would be 25 years before the capacity of this unsuccessful machine would be matched. Although the Titan was operated for many years at a mine in Canada, only one was ever built, as its bulk, sluggish performance, and immense thirst for fuel made it less cost effective than had been expected at the time of its development. Because of the tires available at the time, the Titan also needed three axles, with singles at the front and twinned rubber on the two rear axles, the rearmost of which also featured steering to minimize scrubbing.

The next big successful jump in truck capacity started with Wiseda's KL-2450 in 1982, which established the 240-U.S.-ton/216-tonne class and was followed later with Cat's 793 and Komatsu's 830E. Although significantly larger than the 190-U.S.-ton/171-tonne trucks that had topped the (practical) payload charts previously, these new machines used tires based on established principles. The 240-U.S.-ton/216-tonne class has since grown to dominate in large coal and copper mining operations in particular, with good tire performance a major factor in the size class becoming extremely popular from the 1990s on. But design limits had been reached in terms of the available tire technology with this truck class, and to allow larger

Michelin's XS tire appeared in 1960 and offered a large radial for earthmoving applications with a tread pattern that provided good grip and longevity. *Michelin collection*

The steel bead wire in a tire plays a key role in giving it structural strength as well as durability. To ensure quality, the belting must be clean and free from contaminants that could affect the bonding process. *Michelin collection*

payloads, a different design philosophy had to be followed. One of the main reasons for this was that it was simply not practical to offer a tire with the larger external diameter necessary to permit the jump in payload capability. Such a tire would have been so large that it would have been impossible to transport cost effectively, as it would not be allowed to be carried by either road or rail, due to width restrictions on highways or in tunnels. Clearly, the cost of renting helicopters to airlift each unit around the globe would have been prohibitive. The final nail in the coffin for a larger tire built on conventional principles was the fact that the high pressures required to give it structural support would have presented serious safety issues.

The answer for the earthmoving equipment market came in the form of low-profile technology, a concept that had been developed initially for the automotive sector. Using this approach, the firms were able to develop tires for both trucks and wheel loaders that provided the bigger payload capacities and larger rim sizes required without increasing their external diameter beyond the practical

limits for transport. In 1995, Michelin made what was then the largest radial tire in the world, the 55/80 57 X Mine D2 for Caterpillar's 994 wheel loader. Michelin then made its first low-profile earthmover tires in 1996, although these were not available on the market and were used purely for the firm's own research-and-development program. Working in close partnership with Caterpillar, Michelin came up with the groundbreaking 55/63R63 in 1998, a 63-inch/1.6-meter-size low-profile tire for the giant 797 truck.

But Bridgestone Firestone was not sitting still, responding very quickly with its own tire designs pitched at the same market. Both firms used a similar concept, increasing the load capacity through the use of a wider profile rather than increasing the overall diameter. Just as Caterpillar and Michelin worked together on some tire projects, Bridgestone Firestone and LeTourneau also carried out joint development of new designs. The world's largest tire, the huge Bridgestone Firestone 7757, was designed specifically for the world's largest loader,

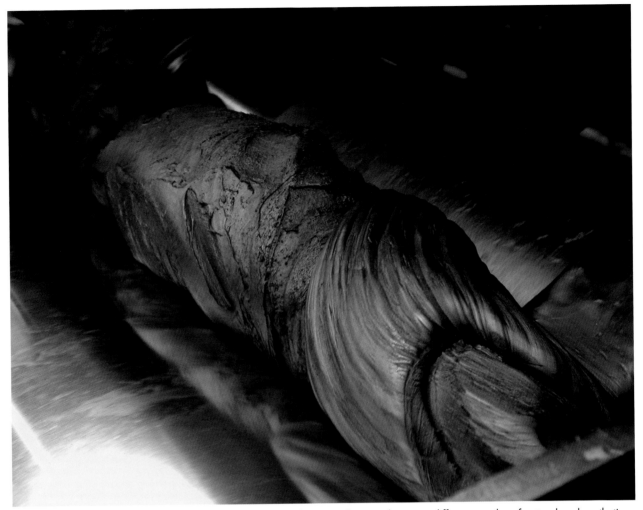

Many different types of rubber are used in a tire, with manufacturers choosing between different grades of natural and synthetic rubbers to provide a tire for a specific duty. Once these have been mixed thoroughly, they are extruded. *Michelin collection*

LeTourneau's mighty L-2350. But reaching the stage of having a finished product required many, many small steps and involved a high level of experience in the complex field of chemical engineering. The Bridgestone Firestone team had to examine the new tire design from the micro level, working with carbon black, silicates, and new chemical agents. A key aim of the project was to reduce tire temperatures by 4 to 5 degrees centigrade and prevent the heat buildups that would result in high wear and early failure. New compounding methods and new construction techniques were able to bring a substantial benefit and were stepping stones toward the radical concept the firm was able to produce in the shape of the 7757 for LeTourneau's L-2350.

Low-profile tires (such as Michelin's 58/80R63) have helped push the boundaries of mine truck technology, as their extra load capacity has allowed manufacturers to make a big jump in payload to the 360–400 U.S. tons/325–360 tonnes now offered by Cat's 797B, Liebherr's T282B, and Unit Rig's MT5500B. Similar tire technology has been equally helpful for Caterpillar's 994 wheel loaders, LeTourneau's L series, and more recently Komatsu's WA1200.

Goodyear's radical two-piece tire provided a very different approach. This had a separate casing and tread that could be mounted together at the mine site. The firm's explanation for the concept was straightforward—the system offered a substantial reduction in transport costs, given the extremely bulky nature of off-highway tires. By removing outside diameter constraints for future tire development, Goodyear reckoned it could offer much higher capacity products and reduce operating costs for its customers. One of the key benefits came from the ability to replace the tread while retaining the same casing at a much lower cost than having to change out the complete tire. This design did not even need any bonding, deriving

Building up the casing of a large earthmover tire is a complex and lengthy process, and care is taken to ensure there is no contamination before moving it to the next stage of the process. *Michelin collection*

When the basic structure of the tire has been assembled, it can be put inside the mold for curing, which heats the rubber and embosses the desired tread pattern. *Michelin collection*

the necessary frictional resistance between tread and casing from air pressure alone. Tests in the dirt showed the tire to offer both stability and traction, even with pressures as low as 5 psi/0.35 bar and without separation occurring. The first 33.00R51 E-4 prototype was run at speeds of 35 miles per hour/55 kilometers per hour and grades of 12 percent on a Cat 785B haul truck, clocking 2,600 hours in the dirt during a two-year development program to prove the concept. The basic benefit of the two-piece tire is that it allows the user to utilize fully the life of the casing. Conventional tires can be retreaded as long as the casing structure is in reasonable condition, and there are a number of specialists in this field offering quality retreads. These tires are far removed from the cheap retreaded tires that flooded the automotive market starting in the 1970s that offered doubtful quality and had a tendency to lose their tread after comparatively short use. Good quality retreads for the earthmoving sector are comparable with the originals, and the best suppliers keep close links with tire manufacturers to ensure the tread patterns and rubber compounds meet the design specifications of the original manufacturers. However, Goodyear's two-piece system cut out the need for this stage, allowing the tire casing to be fitted with a new tread, and this could even be carried out on-site. The projected cost benefits over conventional retreading were substantial, as the Goodyear concept could cut out the need to remove the casing from the truck and take it off-site to a specialist firm to prepare the casing and fit a new tread.

Manufacturers are also looking at an ultra-wide single tire intended to take over for the conventional dual configuration used on rigid haul trucks virtually since their inception. And the next generation of tires for large trucks and wheel loaders is most likely in trials at this very moment. Michelin, for its part, carries out trials at its test facility at Almeria in Spain. The tire development process can lead to some interesting solutions, and Michelin initially tried testing large tires for Cat's 797 using a smaller 793 that was specially modified for the purpose (in effect making it a monster monster truck), but the results were not exactly as had been hoped. As a result, Michelin then spoke with Caterpillar and subsequently took delivery of a 797 truck at the test facility in Almeria, one of the first of these units supplied outside of the Americas. However, peering over the fence is not an option, as access to this site is restricted, and Bridgestone Firestone is equally secretive about its own test area.

To make sure these large tires can do what is expected of them, Bridgestone Firestone, Goodyear, and Michelin (and the other firms) all have to carry out extensive test programs as part of their research and development phases. The machines are quite literally used to pound the dirt and find any design features that require changing prior to putting the products into production. This is no small feat, and Michelin, for example, says it expects test tires to clock up some 1.9 million miles/3 million kilometers per year as it proves new or existing tread types. However, due to the wide array of different operating conditions, earthmoving tires are application specific and the development process is extensive, as it requires an array of products to suit all market needs. For instance, firms have developed tires for existing truck categories that offer a deeper tread design able to maintain speed and thermal capacity but with a pattern and structure intended to achieve a 20 percent greater life.

Once the tire has been heated and cured in the mold for the required period, it takes on the tread pattern, while the mechanical properties of the rubber are also changed. *Michelin collection*

Even when a finished tire reaches the end of the production process, it undergoes a careful visual inspection. A certain number of tires may be taken off-line and examined closely with nondestructive testing equipment. *Michelin collection*

Special equipment is required to handle heavy earthmoving tires during fitting, and this machinery makes the process quicker and safer. To minimize production losses, it is vital to reduce downtime from maintenance chores such as tire replacement.

Keep Rolling Along

Progress has by no means stopped. Technology allows continuous monitoring of tire health and performance on-site, and this was developed to allow large mining operations to optimize cycling of their trucks. Michelin announced its MEMS (Michelin Equipment Management System) system in the mid-1990s, with Bridgestone Firestone also discussing the development of its rival technology around the same time. Not to be outdone, other manufacturers such as Goodyear and Yokohama have since unveiled their own systems as well. The introduction of such technology was not immediate, though, and followed an intensive research-and-development program, requiring several years of testing in the field. The aim of all of these monitoring systems was to achieve greater productivity through being able to implement effective preventative maintenance schedules, increasing overall output, and reducing downtime. The cost issue was a crucial one, considering each 57-inch/1.45-meter rim-size tire for a Cat 994 loader cost around U.S.$30,000, so customers were not keen to replace these units more often than absolutely necessary. By using tire monitoring, customers could detect any pressure problems, such as punctures, and could also anticipate when attention or repairs would be needed so that it could be scheduled in alongside other general truck maintenance tasks. The technology was developed initially for bigger operations using larger machines and can produce impressive cost savings for its users, along with major gains in output. Simpler systems are coming to market for smaller earthmoving machines too, as the cost of the technology reduces gradually in real terms, with similar benefits to the customer or user as seen in large mine trucks and wheel loaders. Tire-monitoring packages could eventually become commonplace for all types of equipment.

Goodyear's two-piece tire offered an interesting alternative to conventional types, as it allowed the user to remove the tread quickly on-site and replace it with another. *Bristol Voss*

Intelligent tire technology offers a vital tool in optimizing tire assets. Fleet managers generally concern themselves with the resulting effects of tire failures, and though they may consider the causes, this all comes after the fact. Vital signals that the tire is going to have a problem are ignored until it is too late, but if these can be caught early on, there are huge potential gains to be made. Tires represent a substantial chunk of total truck-fleet operating costs, and alerting an operation of a potential problem and allowing preventative measures to be taken before they require expensive repairs can protect assets that keep production moving. Intelligent tire technology is intended to capture that early-stage information and ensure that production equipment does not have to go off-line. Tire tag systems are already working throughout the world in many large surface and underground mining applications, with this technology coming down in price gradually, so that it may eventually filter down to users of small construction plants.

A typical system uses a 3-inch/76.2-millimeter tag that is bonded in place inside the tire. The device features a small transponder able to monitor internal pressure and temperature and then feed this data through a transmitter to two types of receivers, either to a site's dispatch software system (at larger mining operations) or to a read-out in the cab. All of the signals the tag sends out are received and logged by the machine's onboard computer and the information can be downloaded for analysis on a PC if required. These monitoring systems check tire status regularly (every three minutes or so), and should the pressure change by 3 psi/0.21 bars or more, or the temperature increase by 41 degrees Fahrenheit/5 degrees Centigrade, the tag boots up and sends the information immediately. If no change is detected in either pressure or temperature, the transmitter will only send a signal every 15 minutes, which helps preserve its battery life. In regular mine operating conditions, the batteries powering the tags will last three to four years and can be reused should they outlast the tires. The accuracy of such a system is plus or minus 2 psi/0.14 bar or plus or minus 37.4 degrees Fahrenheit/3 degrees Centigrade temperature, but it is worth noting that these systems do not eliminate the need for visual inspections, which the tire manufacturers agree should be carried out on a regular basis to look out for surface cuts and other abnormalities.

Maintenance is not the only issue, though. Studies show that tire wear is linked exponentially to the torque that is sent to the ground, so haul-road gradients can also have an effect on life, as a laden truck climbing a slope has to deliver maximum power to the rear wheels. Larger machines generate heavier tire loads, resulting in wear rates that accelerate at exponential levels. It was because of this that manufacturers switched to low-pressure technology for the ultra haulers and loaders, as this approach takes advantage of the links between inflation pressure and tire life. Surprising as it may seem, reduced pressures can boost wear life, as this gives better cut resistance and also reduces the risks of punctures. Because of the lower internal pressure, these tires can actually envelop a fallen rock or item of debris that would puncture a conventional type. It is worth noting, too, that punctures in earthmover tires can be extremely dangerous because of the size of these units, the volume of air they contain, and the pressures involved. In some cases there have been fatalities caused by truck tire blowouts.

The commercial gains to be made in cost/ton by maximizing tire life can be substantial for any earthmoving or rock-hauling duty, whether in mining or construction. Tires can account for as much as 20 percent of haulage costs, with poor working conditions having the ability to make a huge increase in expenses. During the life of a mine truck, the owner is likely to spend as much on tires as on purchasing the machine in the first place.

To keep the accountants happy, tire management and selection are vital. Many of the latest products are application specific with regard to tread and rubber compound, so this has to be factored into the long-term cost equation. Customers can also boost the performance and wear life of each tire by improving site conditions and maintenance practices. The major manufacturers have amassed considerable data from working operations in this respect and have uncovered some shocking facts. Rock cuts have a major impact on costs, and without proper management, a site can even lose as much as 65 percent of its tires to rock cuts. In such a situation, the tires are lost at 60 percent of their potential wear life and are losing 26 percent of their total value, a statistic that would have many sharp-eyed company accountants applying pressure to sack the site manager responsible.

Some sidewall cuts in tires can be repaired and there are numerous kits on the market aimed at this, while there are specialists and tire suppliers offering these repairs as a service. As long as the sidewall cut is not so deep that the steel belting is damaged and the structural integrity of the casing compromised, it is possible that a repair can be made. Rubber around the affected area is cut away and this is then prepared, with the relevant bonding agents and patching material next being applied. Once the patch is properly cured, the repaired section should be virtually as strong as an undamaged sidewall, as long as the process has been carried out correctly with a good quality kit. But, addressing the cause of such problems directly can reap huge rewards, eliminating the need for the repairs in the first place. Taking care to improve haul roads and loading or dumping areas and keeping them free from fallen debris, for instance, can reduce the risk of rock cuts and will most likely lead to an increase in tire life. It is worth noting that mine sites making efficient use of dozers and graders to keep loading and tipping areas, as well as haul roads, free from potholes and clear from debris, tend to have a lower incidence of such tire failures. Similarly, road design can also have an effect. Turns that are excessively sharp or ramps that are too steep will cause additional wear and tear by causing scrubbing on the bends or loss of traction, respectively. Site managers have to keep a wary eye on operating conditions too, as heavy rain, for instance, can make haul roads extremely slippery. This reduces safety levels considerably and increases the risk of the trucks spinning their tires and causing undue wear. In extreme conditions, continuing to operate a truck haul fleet can actually become counter-productive in financial terms. By addressing tire management issues and improving site conditions, one mine was able to decrease its rock-cut rate by 6 percent and increase tire life by 15 percent. The total net savings for one year represented 7 percent of the tire expenses, while the remedial measures were made at minimal cost, which kept the accountants very happy indeed.

Fitting tires correctly is another key stage in maintenance procedures, and it is not simply a case of attaching a tire to a rim and pumping in the required volume of air. Tire manufacturers have strict guidelines on how their products should be fitted, and this is a specialist task. Handling tires from large trucks and wheel loaders for surface mines can be a complicated, expensive, and risky business, particularly considering the size and weight of the biggest units, as well as the air pressures involved. The most effective and safe way to mount, demount, and move these bulky tires from one place to another is to use tire-manipulating equipment made for the job by one of the specialist manufacturers servicing this niche market. These handlers are often built on vehicles designed as fully integrated packages engineered to get the job done reliably and efficiently. In addition to a heavy-duty tire handler, the vehicles come with air systems equipped with industrial cooling and filtration, wireless remote controls, and substantial storage capacity. Such machines can lift tires weighing up to 7 U.S. tons/6.35 tonnes at a radius of 195 inches/4.95 meters. In underground mining there are space considerations to be taken into account given the restricted nature of the operating environment, so more compact tire-handling solutions are required. These tire manipulators are often designed to fit onto conventional telehandlers, adapted with special electronics and catalytic converters for underground mining duties or purpose-built underground mine loaders by means of quick couplers. Articulated booms can be fitted for additional versatility, meaning that just one person is enough to operate the handler, while also providing maneuverability in confined spaces.

Monitoring air pressure can also reap rewards as underinflated tires wear out quickly. Case studies show that even a reasonably run mining operation with 80 percent of its tires within plus or minus 10 percent of recommended life will still lose some 8 percent of its tire value. Accurate air-pressure management can provide an effective solution and should be carried out daily, or at the very least weekly. Carrying out these checks using existing personnel adds nothing to the expense of running a site but can easily save up to 5 percent in costs. However, continuous checks are ideal, and this is one of the driving factors behind tire chip technology. The risks from ignoring this are substantial, triggering potential health and safety issues as well as causing costs to skyrocket. Allowing pressure to drop below recommended levels in a tire causes overheating, and the greater the pressure drop, the greater the heating effect. This happens because an underinflated tire flexes more than it has been designed to do, with friction being generated in both the tread and sidewall. For example, taking a thin piece of metal and bending it back and forward repeatedly will cause it to fatigue and eventually break. At the point where it fails, friction generated by the bending action will also cause the broken edges to heat up. While rubber is elastic, there are limits to its capabilities,

and if it overheats, its material properties will be compromised and failures can and will occur. Underinflated tires are highly prone to punctures and other early failures, as the extra stresses imposed by excessive flexing and the additional heat generated damages their structure. Overheated tires can also catch fire internally, and this is not always immediately visible, adding to the dangers involved. If the tire fire is not caught very quickly, a truck can rapidly become an inferno, and once this occurs, there is very little chance of dousing the flames. When a truck fire catches hold, the only thing to do is to stand at a safe distance and watch the machine burn out. Clearly, this is a crucial safety issue, and no mine would want to lose an operator to a tire fire, nor would the firm's accountants, lawyers, and insurers want to have to deal with the aftermath of a fatal accident.

In evaluating the long-term benefits of one type of tire over another, monitoring is crucial, and firms have had to come up with new and more accurate ways of measuring tire performance. Partly, they have achieved this using the real-time monitoring systems mentioned earlier. However, statistical analysis is also used. In the past, mines have achieved this with fairly simplistic methods of monitoring the behavior of and looking at the results gained by different brands or tread patterns on a yearly basis. Such a general method can overlook many of the uncontrollable variables that occur in real working situations, which can skew the results.

One variable is introduced by new technology. If new compounds or new patterns are introduced in the fleet in the middle of the year, the performance results will be distorted. Seasonal factors can have a similar distorting effect, as the hotter months of the year will generally decrease tire performance. It takes no great depth of knowledge to see that the hotter the ambient temperature, the hotter the tire runs, and this affects all aspects of its general performance. A hot tire is more prone to a rock cut and more prone to wear. Changes to operating conditions and mine plans can also have a major impact, with road design, grade changes, new cuts in new areas of the mine, and even different operators all impacting performance.

Well Made

Quality of manufacture is key to long-term tire reliability, with cleanliness an essential factor. The manufacturing process has to eliminate dirt contamination because this prevents materials from adhering to each other. Similarly, thorough checks are made more or less continuously throughout the tire manufacturing process to ensure that the quality of materials, process temperatures, and material properties all lie within the strict tolerances required.

By using Goodyear's two-piece tire, customers could effectively cut out the need for retreading while maximizing utilization from the casing. *Bristol Voss*

There are a number of main components, the most obvious of which is rubber. However, carbon black, antioxidants, oils, and vulcanizers also have important roles to play, while steel is of course required for the belting. Using the carbon black makes the rubber hard wearing and allows it to flex easily for much longer periods. Antioxidants give protection from ultraviolet light and prevent material degradation over the life of the tire that would otherwise lead to rapid surface wear and early replacement. Oils make the rubber more plastic and improve the mixing process, while the vulcanizers accelerate the curing process and are added last of all.

Mixing of the materials has to occur at the right times, with temperatures carefully monitored at each stage to ensure that the desired properties will be achieved once the tires are finished. Once the tire manufacturing process

Next page: Good, clean haul roads that are maintained regularly can have a major impact on tire life. By ensuring that spillage is cleaned up quickly and that potholes are smoothed over, equipment users can reduce risks of sidewall cuts or punctures. *Jonathan Watt*

starts, the clock is ticking too, as some of the materials can only be left at certain stages for relatively short periods, so the whole process has to be managed carefully to maximize quality and minimize wastage. Uncured rubber has a shelf life, which for a natural rubber can vary from 8 hours to 15 days, so the production management process is crucial in maximizing efficiency and minimizing wastage.

As large tires for the biggest earthmoving machines are complex units requiring an involved manufacturing process with up to 80 separate production steps, running a factory efficiently is a huge logistical exercise. The operation begins with raw rubber being loaded onto the feed conveyors and carefully weighed to ensure that the mix is correct. Up to three different grades of natural rubbers may be mixed together to provide a uniform quality and these come from several sources such as Brazil, Nigeria, or Indonesia. Synthetic rubbers are fed simultaneously onto parallel conveyors, as these provide different properties that are useful in specific duties. Tire manufacturers balance the mix between natural and synthetic rubbers depending on the application intended. The rule of thumb in this regard is that machines that travel at higher speeds for comparatively long runs, such as mine trucks, generate higher temperatures in their tires. Therefore, they require a larger content of the more heat-resistant natural rubbers to prevent early failures. Meanwhile, slower-moving machines such as wheel loaders have tires containing higher percentages of synthetic rubbers to give good cut resistance and maximize durability.

Depending on the application, the mix of natural and synthetic rubbers and other chemicals is matched precisely to maintain optimum quality. The mixed rubbers are heated to temperatures of 170 degrees centigrade, and this material comes out of the mixer in batches that are then rolled into sheets and cut into plaques that are easy to handle. The plaques are stacked on top of each other automatically, and small samples are taken to ensure that mixing has been carried out properly. These plaques are chopped up once more, then squeezed out through an extruder and reheated to make them plastic, before heading off for a rolling process in which the temperature is carefully controlled. Once this is complete, the material is cut into sections and laid on aluminum sheets, ready for use in the actual tire-making process, with tags added to each batch

Because of the nature of some sites, higher tire wear may be inevitable despite the best efforts of the site manager. Quarries or mines that combine steep ramps with hard rock and large amounts of clay underfoot place higher stresses on tires.

to help track product quality. Continuous checking is required on the production line and in the lab to ensure that the material is homogenous and that the carbon black, antioxidants, oils, and vulcanizers have each been added at the right time to achieve the best quality.

There are two basic categories of rubber—for tread and sidewalls—but the supply situation is a complex one. Manufacturers have up to 200 different compounds to choose from, and these are all mixed and matched to the application and duty cycle.

While it is feasible for the manufacturing process for car and other relatively small tires to be automated, this would not be practical for large earthmover products, as these may be made in relatively low volumes. As such, there is a high degree of manual input, and all of the rubber layers are put on basically by hand, with the basis for the tire built up around a drum. This is a highly skilled process, as the operators have to make sure that no air becomes trapped between the pieces of rubber, which would affect quality and would quickly lead to problems in use. Different manufacturers may have different approaches, but in general, making the casing and tread for an earthmover tire first requires separate operations, with the two components then put together, checked for size and shape, and finally moved over for molding.

When the tire is conformed, but still minus its tread or sidewall marking, it can be fitted into the mold, at which point heat and pressure are applied. This stage changes the physical properties and mechanical characteristics of the rubber, making it elastic instead of plastic.

Manufacturers do have different techniques, but in general, cure times can range from 90 minutes for the smaller tires up to 10 hours for the largest products aimed at giant trucks and wheel loaders. Quality is checked at this stage, too, and as soon as the tires come out of the molds, they are examined closely. Visual inspections are useful at this point, with accurate weighing of the products. Spot checks may also be made on a certain percentage of the tires, using the latest ultrasonic detection systems and x-ray equipment. All in all, the manufacturing focus is on producing a quality product that will not fail unexpectedly, whatever the name on the tire.

With different operations having different conditions, performance can benefit from using application-specific tires. Manufacturers have developed tires for long hauls and high speeds or for highly abrasive conditions with steep climbs and a high risk of sidewall cuts, for instance.

ALL-WHEEL DRIVE
A VERSATILE EARTHMOVING TOOL

With their all-wheel drive and high-flotation capabilities, articulated dump trucks (ADTs) have become a common sight on all sorts of off-highway operations, offering users the ability to carry a full load in poor ground conditions. The machines have two chassis components joined by an articulation hitch, with the front section housing the engine, gearbox, cab, and driver and the rear section supporting the body used to carry dirt or rock. Chassis articulation gives the trucks good steering and terrain-following capabilities, and having power to all wheels means the machines can drive through poor ground conditions without bogging down. Mines, quarries, and construction sites all use ADTs because these machines can keep on running in conditions that would halt other types of equipment. Rigid trucks may offer vast payloads in comparison to ADTs, but when the going gets tough, all-wheel drive gets going.

In terms of overall operating efficiency, though, the ADT does not always score as highly as its sales success would suggest. In some respects, the biggest weakness of an ADT is also its strongest feature. The go-anywhere capability of its all-wheel drive is achieved through a complex driveline that requires regular maintenance and limits its top speed to 30 miles per hour/50 kilometers per hour or so. Conventional rigid trucks with rear-wheel drive are cheaper to run and maintain, offer travel speeds of up to 40–50 miles per hour/65–80 kilometers per hour, and, of course, can have maximum capacities that make an ADT's

Volvo's twin-axle 631 truck was the first production model from the firm and appeared in 1963. Its design was highly influential and set the pattern for later Volvo ADTs. However, the machine still had drive at the front only, which limited its rough-terrain performance.

The early Moxy trucks had very square-shaped cab designs that look old-fashioned now, but these machines were extremely innovative in their day. Their rough-terrain performance in particular was unequaled for many years.

full payload look almost as insubstantial as a wheelbarrow by comparison. Meanwhile, for a short dirt haul, the scraper is by far the most efficient earthmoving tool.

The advantage of the ADT is its sheer versatility. It is a jack-of-all-trades machine for hauling material where nothing else can move. This is why the ADT has become so important for hauling dirt and rock. The ADT can be used in a wide array of duties and applications, while six-wheel drive ensures good traction even in the worst operating conditions. If bad weather means that an ADT bogs down on-site, it is arguable the conditions are so poor that operation is unlikely to be cost-effective and that work should also stop on safety grounds.

In developing countries with high rainfall levels, for instance, the ADT offers perhaps the best haulage option. In comparison with dedicated rigid trucks with large capacities, ADTs are cheap and, partnered with hydraulic excavators, can allow effective mining operations to start up with relatively low capital investment. Furthermore, ADTs are well suited to the contracting sector for construction, quarrying, and mining operations and can be

bought and sold relatively quickly because they also have a ready market. Contractors have even modified ADTs for use in underground mining, requesting basic modifications from manufacturers such as lowered cabs and cut-down headboards, additional lighting, revised electronics, and catalytic converters for the exhaust system.

The success of the ADT has made a further impact on the scraper market, which has never really recovered from the slump in orders during the 1970s as the number and scale of the world's highway building projects began to dry up. While Caterpillar and Terex still make motor scrapers, both firms realized long ago that their ADT products were much larger-volume sellers. There have been attempts to make all-wheel-drive rigid trucks too, which have chipped away at the corners of the ADT sector. Komatsu experimented with a curious machine some years ago using hydrostatic drive at the front and conventional mechanical drive at the rear that offered a 61-U.S.-ton/55-tonne payload. Intended largely for use in some of Japan's quarries, many of which feature steep hauls, the Komatsu machine was interesting technically if ultimately commercially unsuccessful. And of course, there was also the Payhauler 350C, a 50–55-U.S.-ton/45–45-tonne truck developed originally by International in the 1960s and now part of the Terex stable. With its twinned tires, the Payhauler is a niche market machine aimed at landfill operations, countries with high rainfall levels, and a few quarries with steep ramps. However, Terex now concentrates on supplying spares for the 350C and rebuilding old units. There is a new small 4WD rigid truck on the market in the shape of Randon's 30-U.S.-ton/27-tonne-capacity RK430C, which the Brazilian firm has developed over many years from a much earlier Kockums design. The RK430C is powered by a 333-horsepower/248-kilowatt Scania diesel driving through an Eaton transmission.

Although these all-wheel-drive rigid trucks have not made much of a dent in ADT sales, not everyone is convinced by the articulated truck concept. Some big truck users are skeptical of the production advantages offered by ADTs and question the cost-effectiveness of these much smaller machines, given their payload limitations and high driveline-maintenance requirements.

Destination Moon

As these machines only appeared in the post-World War II period, you'd think that determining who built the first ADT would be easy. But you'd be wrong, and this is, in fact, a topic of some debate. There are various claims that machines built in the United States and the United Kingdom could be classed as ADTs. Some of these used the front end of a scraper hooked up to a purpose-built dump body at the rear, and the Athey Corporation was one of several firms building such machines in the late 1940s. In 1952, Wooldridge adapted its existing Cummins-powered scraper by fitting a dump body that featured a curious sliding mechanism, creating an articulated hauler with a 19-cubic-yard/15-cubic-meter load. But whether these scraper-derived machines can be classed as true ADTs is a matter of opinion.

One strong contender for the first ADT was built in Sweden. In 1959, the enterprising Swedish tractor manufacturer Bolinder-Munktell put together a simple truck body with vertical sides mounted on four wheels. This body was attached, via an articulating joint, to a tractor with its

Bell first began building proper ADTs in the early 1980s, and even after some years of development, their roots from the firm's rugged industrial tractors could still be seen in the early 1990s. *Bell collection*

For many years, the two larger DJB/Caterpillar ADTs were distinctive because they featured a cab that was offset, and this configuration allowed a short forward chassis design.

front axle removed. As with a modern ADT, the steering was by hydraulic ram, though the only drive was from the tractor's remaining axle, now at the front of the machine. In tune with the spirit of the time, this machine was called the Moon Rocket, but despite its unlikely name, it made an impression. Based in the city of Eskilstuna, Bolinder-Munktell had been in business for many years making agricultural tractors and had become a subsidiary of Volvo some time earlier. (Although the full Bolinder-Munktell name was dropped in the early 1970s, the Volvo off-highway machines continued to be bear the Volvo BM marque for many years.)

After testing its prototype, Volvo decided to enter into the ADT business proper, which led directly to the ADTs we know today. The first articulated hauler in series production to bear the Volvo name was the DR631, which made its debut in the early 1960s and featured the distinctive slope-sided dump body that is now the norm in the marketplace. But the DR631 still had front-wheel drive only, and the heritage of its tractor-derived front end could clearly be seen. Whether this machine has any greater

claim to being an ADT than the scraper-derived designs, such as those from the Athey Corporation or Wooldridge, is still argued today. In 1968, though, came Volvo BM's DR860, which featured three axles, articulated steering, 6x4 drive, and would basically set the trend for ADT design as it is today. Many DR860s still survive, and some are even in occasional use.

Caterpillar was another early player in the ADT market through the efforts of U.K. engineering specialist and entrepreneur David Brown. He saw the potential for a versatile truck with all-wheel drive and started building his own, using Caterpillar engines and axles. Brown's original DJB models featured twin axles, and there were models with payloads of 25 and 30 U.S. tons/23 and 27 tonnes, though three-axle machines were developed later. Brown was a real pioneer, pushing the boundaries of truck payload capacity as well as introducing innovative design concepts.

However, it is worth noting that there is a third contender that is often overlooked amongst the claims of being the first ADT. In 1949, Portland, Oregon–based Eddie and Elmer Wagner developed their first articulating

The novel rear-drive configuration used on the Moxy ADTs and the newer Hydrema machine offers some benefits on ground that undulates sharply.

The side-mounted cab on the DJB/Cat D350 and D400 ADTs was influenced heavily by scraper design and had the benefit of making reversing up to a loading tool on the left side easier.

wheel loader with four-wheel drive and then went on to build a true underground loader, the MS-b, in 1958. This was followed soon after by the MS-i, an articulating truck capable of carrying a 10-ton/9-tonne load that was 8 feet/2.4 meters wide, 22 feet/6.7 meters long, and 60 inches/1.52 meters high. While the MS-i was a compact machine aimed at underground mining applications, it certainly offered all-wheel drive on an articulating chassis prior to anything from the Volvo stable.

And if there is such a thing as an afterlife, it's likely the indomitable David Brown is arguing with the Wagner brothers and some departed Bolinder-Munktell personnel as to who was the real father of the articulated truck. What is clear is that the modern ADT developed mainly (if not exactly exclusively) in northern Europe—in Sweden, Norway, and the United Kingdom.

The other of the pioneering firms in the ADT sector was the Norwegian firm Moxy. And while Moxy makes no claims to having been the first to make an ADT, there is less debate over its assertion at having been the pioneer in marketing a true six-wheel-drive machine. This was a real achievement, as there was little in the way of available drive-line componentry suited to the rigors of the off-highway application at the time. The engineers who developed these first units got around this problem by taking a sideways look at other off-highway equipment and opted to use a driveline similar to that seen on some graders, with a single rear differential connected by conventional half shafts to gears that power the wheels. With the gears running encased in an oil bath in large casings, this configuration is still a design feature of the Moxy trucks today.

It took a while for this six-wheel-drive machine to appear though. The founder of Moxy, Birger Hatlebakk, started working on a hauler in 1969 and rolled out his first prototype in 1970. The machine he built was very simple indeed and, like the Bolinder-Munktell machine a decade earlier, used a tractor (a Ford 5000 in this instance) at the front hooked up to a trailer with hydraulic tipping at the rear, offering a 17-U.S.-ton/15-tonne payload. However, the D20 he built later that year was a proper articulated hauler, featuring a box-like cab that was mounted to the left side of the engine on the front chassis. It only had two axles, but the D20 had a 22-U.S.-ton/20-tonne payload and was considerably more sophisticated than the crude machine Hatlebakk had assembled a few months earlier.

The cab offset in the old D300 and D250 Caterpillar-branded ADTs was considerably less pronounced than with the two larger models in the lineup.

With the Moxy trucks, the design of the rear suspension made the brake drums integral with the bogie units, although the firm now offers disc brakes on more recent models.

It is worth noting, though, that the first six-wheel-drive machine was not in fact developed by Hatlebakk's firm. The three axle, all-wheel-drive truck was the product of another Norwegian company called Óveraasen Maskin, based in Gjøvik, and appeared in 1972. Having seen this machine and recognized its potential, Hatlebakk bought the rights to the design in 1973. Appropriately enough with its Norwegian roots, the truck was called the Viking D15 and it offered a 17-U.S.-ton/15-tonne payload, with 36 of these machines built. The D15 paved the way for future Moxy trucks and was replaced in the lineup in 1975 by the 18-U.S.-ton/16-tonne-capacity D16, followed by the uprated D16B in 1977 and then the D16B Super in 1981, by which time the ADT was out of its infancy.

Just Drive

With Moxy having set a lead by offering six-wheel drive, Volvo BM and DJB, as well as a handful of other ADT pioneers, soon realized they had to follow too. Having seen their own haulers clocking up hours in the dirt, the engineers at DJB and Volvo knew that providing maximum traction was crucial if this new class of haul truck was to prove a worthwhile alternative to existing machines like the rigid-chassis truck or the scraper (which neither company made). Experience had already shown that with front-wheel drive only, the twin-axle Athey machines and early Volvo units had serious shortcomings with regard to traction in wet conditions. While wide tires gave reasonable flotation, performance was limited on a steep or slippery haul road, and it was questionable whether or not these machines had any benefits over conventional rigid trucks. The 6x4-driveline-layout Volvo used on its DR860 (and Terex's 2364 introduced in the early 1980s) was better for flotation because of the three axles and for traction because of the multiwheel drive. But Volvo recognized that even its relatively advanced DR860 was a short-term compromise in terms of design, brought about by the lack of suitable off-the-shelf axle components.

It is no secret that manufacturers routinely look at machines built by their rivals, in part to seek design inspiration and in part to ensure that future models will have performance that at least matches, and preferably beats, the competition. Engineers from DJB and Volvo probably cast critical eyes over Moxy's D15 and its novel driveline.

The bogies on the Moxy truck fit directly onto the axle and can swivel through a relatively wide angle, allowing the wheels to follow uneven ground.

Volvo's A35 paved the way for the A40, and though the firm was an ADT pioneer, it arrived relatively late into the market for a 40-U.S.-ton/36-tonne truck.

Terex's C-series ADTs of the mid-1990s were the last to bear the distinctive green color scheme, a reminder of the firm's previous link with Euclid.

Power for the D15's rear wheels was transmitted via a universal joint and through a conventional propshaft to the single rear axle, with gears transferring power to the wheels. There were certainly benefits to this system, as Moxy was (and is still) keen to point out. The fact that the gear casings were able to pivot about the ends of the rear axle provided excellent capabilities on uneven ground. It enabled the tires to remain exactly in line with each other on even the worst terrain, allowing an even contact patch for the tires that maximized traction and reduced the risk of one of the tires spinning out. (Even after years of ADT development from many manufacturers, the rough-terrain performance of a Moxy truck is hard to beat.) But Moxy's rivals decided there were shortcomings with this layout, claiming that the gear drives lowered the overall mechanical efficiency of the system as a whole and soaked up some power from the engine. Worse still, the early Moxy machines suffered from driveline problems when used on rocky sites, as the bulky gear casings could bash against rocks at speed. If such a hammering continued unchecked, the casings cracked. This allowed the internal oil-bath lubrication to seep away, leaving the drive gears to run dry and wear out the teeth very rapidly. Moxy addressed the problem later by increasing the strength of

the casings in the most vulnerable areas, and the later models also had more ground clearance.

First Volvo BM and then DJB decided that if six-wheel drive was necessary to make the ADT a successful product, using two axles at the rear was the way ahead (though DJB persisted with its four-wheel-drive models too). There were difficulties with this, of course, not the least of which was the lack of a suitable heavy-duty axle with a through-drive feature allowing it to transfer power to the third axle. The engineers were also probably aware that having twin live axles at the rear of the truck would lead to the tires lying at different angles to each other in very bad conditions, resulting in uneven contact patches and slightly less traction than was possible with the Moxy system. In spite of these difficulties, though, the engineers persisted. After all, rigid-chassis vehicles with three axles and all-wheel drive had been used as dump trucks and by the military for years by that time, so there was surely a way to transfer power effectively to the third axle in line. And the military had also shown that trucks with all-wheel drive on a three-axle layout could handle tough terrain (the French Army had first used four-wheel-drive trucks in World War I).

Volvo was able to tailor the components it needed to the purpose at hand and managed to introduce a six-wheel-drive

Above and left: The twin-axle Thwaites ADTs offered a reasonable performance and were modern, conventional designs, but, like some of the other small trucks developed, these failed to attract sufficient buyers.

Bell's ejector truck featured heavy-duty chains that were used to move the ejection plate back and forward, rather than by hydraulic ram, as with the Cat machine. *Bell collection*

machine relatively quickly. But for DJB, there was a greater problem, and it took longer for the firm to develop six-wheel-drive ADTs, during which time it persisted with its four-wheel-drive machines only. The DJB ADTs were built around off-the-shelf Caterpillar components, including engines, axles, and transmissions. Caterpillar was less than happy about this situation, because it regarded the DJB ADTs as competition for the Cat rigid trucks and scrapers. As a result, the chances of Caterpillar agreeing to tailor a through-drive axle purely for DJB's needs were nonexistent. The answer for DJB came with a somewhat-complex driveline arrangement using separate shafts for the two rear axles. More complex it may have been, but it worked. What is certain is that the driveline DJB fitted to its three-axle, six-wheel-drive D250, which used the transmission and axles from a Caterpillar wheel loader, was robust and could stand up to hard use.

During the 1970s and early 1980s, sales of ADTs, primarily from DJB, Moxy, and Volvo, grew steadily in Europe. The Caterpillar executives soon realized that David Brown, a bluff Yorkshireman, was not going to give up building ADTs and that such machines were selling in steady numbers in the United Kingdom, Norway, and Sweden. As a result, Caterpillar decided to enter negotiations with Brown rather than try to convince what was still

To modify ADTs for underground use, manufacturers such as Bell, Terex, and Volvo generally fit low-height cabs and cut down the headboard at the front of the dump body to allow better clearance in low-headroom areas. *Bell collection*

a niche market that rigid trucks or scrapers were the only solution to hauling dirt. An arrangement was reached in which DJB would build articulated trucks exclusively for Caterpillar under a license agreement—a deal handled by then junior Caterpillar executive Glen Barton, later to become CEO of the firm. The manufacturing partnership was of huge benefit to both parties. Caterpillar was reluctant to enter the ADT market directly with products developed in-house, as the firm was still not convinced of the long-term potential for these machines. The partnership deal was a low-risk strategy that spared Caterpillar the development costs for a new product line. And by helping DJB improve product quality, Caterpillar gave its dealers an acceptable machine to sell alongside its wheel loaders and newly developed excavator line. Meanwhile, the arrangement meant DJB was able to buy all the Caterpillar engines, transmissions, and axles it needed, effectively as an in-house manufacturer, with the chance to build more ADTs than ever before to supply through the Cat dealer network. That Caterpillar had hydraulic excavators in the range, too, gave its dealers an edge in the

market, and it would be many years before other ADT firms would be in a similar position.

The next major players to enter the ADT market were Terex and Bell, which had observed the sales success being achieved by DJB, Moxy, and Volvo, and decided they wanted a piece of the action. Terex and Bell started working on ADT designs in the early 1980s, developing their machines at more or less the same time but entirely separately at their factories in Scotland and South Africa, respectively. Production models were then launched by Terex and Bell in the mid-1980s, though early types from both firms suffered shortcomings in terms of reliability.

Bell had been making rugged tractors for use in mining, quarrying, and construction duties for some years that were used to pull dump bodies. Like Volvo and Moxy before it, Bell's progression from tractor-based haulers to developing an ADT range was a logical step. The first-generation Bell trucks had twin axles and they had their teething problems, though these were ironed out by the time the firm's three-axle models were rolled out. Bell further improved its three-axle ADTs with its beefed-up B-series

The Bell B50 offered a 50-U.S.-ton/45-tonne payload, but careful engineering on Bell's part ensured that the truck offered a power-to-weight ratio similar to its siblings. *Jonathan Watt*

The rear suspension design of an ADT has to allow for considerable axle movement to cope with rough terrain, while designers also have to ensure that the long travel does not mean wheels will strike the body.

models (and has continued to improve its designs with each successive generation).

Terex's early 2364 was a 23-U.S.-ton/21-tonne-payload ADT with six wheels and drive to four of those, hence the nomenclature, but this model failed to set the market alight. However, a proper 6WD model, the 2366 (again with a 23-U.S.-ton/21-tonne payload), had the traction that customers by now expected and helped build a foundation for Terex in the market. Like Bell, Terex went through a considerable learning curve with its ADT designs, and the B-series models were a vast improvement over the original designs. Another change for the Terex trucks was the switch from air-cooled Deutz engines to liquid-cooled diesels. Though durable (as long as the operators remembered to jet-wash any accumulated dirt from the cooling fins at the end of a shift) and reasonably fuel-efficient, the Deutz engines had the unfortunate effect of heating up the cab, which didn't make those early Terex ADTs popular with operators. When Terex switched to Cummins power units for the 25- and 30-U.S.-ton/23- and 27-tonne-payload machines and the Detroit Diesel S60 engine for its 40-U.S.-ton/36-tonne truck, operators probably heaved a sigh of relief—they no longer had to rely on a regular supply of cold drinks on hot days.

Komatsu had also been watching the development of the ADT sector with some interest. As its archrival Caterpillar had a tie-up with DJB, Komatsu decided to establish its own partnership deal and settled on Moxy. At first this arrangement was very loose, with some dealers, such as Marubeni in the United Kingdom, agreeing to sell the Moxy trucks alongside Komatsu's excavators and wheel loaders. Komatsu-branded Moxy ADTs were also available in Japan. When Moxy's parent, the Brown Group, collapsed in 1990 following a slump in the construction market, Komatsu and the Norwegian government acted to buy up Moxy (other parts of the Brown Group, such as Hymac excavators, Broyt quarry shovels, and Parker crushers, were bought by a number of firms). The Norwegian government held a 90 percent stake in Moxy through its state-owned mining firm Olivin, while Komatsu bought the remaining 10 percent share and agreed to help with new model development, sending design engineers to work on these projects.

Meanwhile, other moves had been occurring in the ADT sector. Danish firm Hydrema had by now complemented its backhoe loader line with a compact, twin-axle ADT offering an 11-U.S.-ton/10-tonne capacity, and this dependable little machine soon proved to sell strongly into

Next page: The first Cat ejector trucks were developed by a contractor using old D400s, and Caterpillar was so impressed with the concept that it worked with the firm to produce an improved model, still using the sturdy D400 as a base.

Further refinement of Caterpillar's ejector trucks has slimmed down the unladen weight, so these machines offer payloads comparable to conventional tipping trucks.

plant hire and tunneling markets. JCB introduced two small, twin-axle ADTs in the late 1980s with side-mounted cabs and very square-shaped front ends. Though durable enough, these models were not a success, as they had high unladen weights for their payload, and the machines were dropped from the range. Aveling Barford was better known for its rigid quarry trucks and, after showing a prototype at various exhibitions, introduced two ADTs, the RXD25 and the RXD28, in 1989. While there was nothing particularly wrong with the Cummins-powered Aveling Barford models, they came as new machine orders were plummeting due to a slump in the construction industry. The Aveling Barford designs failed to catch on and were eventually dropped. The small British firm Haulamatic had scored a deal to supply the British Army with ADTs, but found it hard to compete in the construction market given the poor state of the industry in the early 1990s, and then joined forces with the U.K. rigid truck builder Heathfield. Renamed Heathfield Haulamatic, this firm struggled to remain in business and soon stopped building

either ADTs or rigid trucks, its sales operation eventually bought up by Bell when it first decided to enter the European market.

Also in the early 1990s, Gordon Brown, previously the owner of the Brown Group, joined forces with other businessmen to set up a new and somewhat smaller ADT design and manufacturing business called DDT. This firm may have been small, but it set design precedents that other firms were to follow and develop further. DDT's innovation was to offer a truck with an ejector-type body (DDT stood for discharge dump truck) instead of using a conventional tipping body. The firm marketed this strongly on its safety merits as a machine that was far less likely to roll over on-site if dumping a load on soft or uneven ground. It was certainly a novel idea for the ADT sector, though ejector bodies had already been used in underground mining trucks for many years to cope with height restrictions in confined spaces. The DDT ejector truck designs drew a good deal of comment, though sales were at best sluggish, and the

Like other haulers, ADTs are designed with bodies that allow for clean material ejection during tipping, with engineers having to model the way dirt flows from the body almost as liquids do through a spout.

firm then developed models with conventional tipping bodies, which seemed to find more customers.

As time passed, ADT sales grew, and the Caterpillar-branded line became very successful, becoming a major force in this market segment and second only to Volvo in terms of overall market share. In 1996, Caterpillar decided the time was right to make the further move of buying the articulated truck business, by then called Artix, along with the rights to the design and the factory at Peterlee in the United Kingdom, from David Brown. One of the benefits of the acquisition was that Caterpillar was now able to design components specifically for its own ADTs.

Around the same time, site dumper manufacturer Thwaites introduced two small twin-axle trucks, with capacities of 12 and 16 U.S. tons/11 and 14.4 tonnes. The smaller model was not articulated and had steering axles, so technically it wasn't an ADT, although the larger machine had center articulation. Neither was successful, though, and these machines faded from the firm's range.

After some good years, the successful partnership between Komatsu and Moxy fell apart in the late 1990s. Without knowing from the executives exactly why Komatsu opted to sell its 10 percent stake in Moxy, it is possible to make some educated guesses. At one point, it did seem as if Komatsu would buy the 90 percent share of Moxy held by the state-owned mining firm Olivin. Komatsu was certainly interested in the Moxy product line but was probably not so keen on the Moxy factory, despite its being situated in a picturesque area on the Norwegian coastline. Komatsu had extensive manufacturing capacity in Europe by then and it seems likely Komatsu would have wanted to shift ADT production to one of its other European plants. At the time, both Komatsu's excavator factory at Birtley in the United Kingdom (a site which had previously belonged to Caterpillar and had been used originally to build scrapers) or the former Hanomag wheel loader facility at Hanover in Germany would have probably had the capacity for an ADT line. For its part, the Norwegian government would not have been keen to see jobs in a state-owned business go overseas following a sell-off of the Moxy brand. However, it was no secret that Komatsu had also managed to accumulate considerable engineering expertise with regard to ADTs during its tie-up with Moxy, and it came as no surprise when, a few years later, Komatsu rolled out its own models. What is perhaps surprising is that the Japanese-designed Komatsu ADTs bore almost no resemblance to the Moxy trucks.

Back in the United Kingdom, DDT had been struggling to compete against tough competition and sold out its product line to Case New Holland, which promptly shifted production to the Astra rigid truck factory in Italy. The ejector trucks (which had never sold well and suffered from seized ejector rams in cold weather or hard use) were dropped, and the product focus centered on the conventional tipping body models, which were developed and improved considerably.

It is not clear when the BelAZ ADT, built in Belarus, was first launched, but this model has only been offered in Commonwealth of Independent States (CIS) countries so far. The firm is best known for its rigid trucks, while the front end of its 40-U.S.-ton/36-tonne-class 7528 ADT appears to bear a resemblance to the models from the company's own scraper line. Five-speed transmissions are fitted with a Detroit Diesel rated at 542 horsepower/404 kilowatts (though there has been a choice of Deutz, Cummins, or Russian TMZ engines).

Over the years, various names have come and gone from the ADT market, such as Aveling Barford, Camill, Faun, Haulamatic, Hudson, Morley, Nordverk, Northfield, Shawnee-Poole, and Whitlock. But the sector continues to flourish, with other firms having entered and, in JCB's case, re-entered the sector too. Of the ADTs on the market now, the major manufacturers—Bell, Caterpillar, Terex, and Volvo—all use three axles for their 6WD designs (though Volvo, for one, offers a special twin-axle model). Moreover, when Komatsu introduced its own-design ADT models, these also came with three axles in spite of the firm's earlier partnership with Moxy. And of the other ADT builders offering three-axle machines, such as Randon, CNH/Linkbelt, BelAZ, and JCB, only Danish firm Hydrema has followed Moxy's lead by using the grader-inspired rear-gear-drive configuration (Hydrema still makes its small, twin-axle truck too).

ADTs have to be matched carefully to the loading machine to ensure optimum productivity. The bucket size of the wheel loader or excavator should be sufficient to allow it to fill the ADT's body in an optimum number of passes.

In the United Kingdom and some other countries, ADTs are often fitted with high-volume bodies for coal hauling. While larger rigid trucks are used for shifting overburden, the United Kingdom's relatively high rainfall levels and small surface mines make it efficient to use ADTs as production haulers.

Just Go

In spite of their go-anywhere abilities, ADTs have not always won friends and influenced people. All-wheel drive requires mechanical complexity, and it is no surprise that driveline problems have long been a bugbear for ADTs, with, in most instances, six-wheel drive, a forward-mounted engine, and power transmitted equally to the rear via an articulation joint. Moreover, the components operate in a harsh environment, and in an unforgiving duty cycle at that. Using the engineer's rule of thumb that any inherently complex design will inevitably suffer technical problems, it's no surprise that the driveline is so often the Achilles heel of an ADT. Sophisticated computer design technology may make it easier to eliminate such problems during research and development, but owing to the nature of engineering methodology, weaknesses sometimes are overlooked. However, the fact that the latest machines now feature smart electronics constantly controlling and monitoring performance makes it far easier to track down problems and solve them quickly.

Advances in driveline technologies have brought huge performance advantages, with limited-slip differentials more or less standard for the ADT sector. Developments such as lockable differentials and sealed-in drivelines have further improved performance. On some new machines the differentials can be locked while the machines are moving at speeds of up to 12.5 miles per hour/20 kilometers per hour, with 100 percent lock-up on all wheels to improve traction in the wet. There is no longer the need to stop the truck to engage the differential locks, which vastly reduces the risk of a machine losing traction and bogging down should the ground be particularly soft or slippery. Other features include electronic clutch controls that eliminate wheel slip.

And with features like sealed-in drivelines and performance monitoring, new ADTs offer longer component life and reduced downtime for maintenance, making them longer lasting and cheaper to run than before. By selecting lubrication oils carefully and increasing scheduled driveline maintenance to 5,000 hours, the service costs for some

When an ADT is used for coal hauling, it is usually necessary to fit a tailgate to prevent spillage, as the lighter weight of the load allows it to be piled higher in the body than with earth or rock.

new-generation ADTs are much reduced. Maintained properly, an ADT should last for around 12,000 to 15,000 operating hours or so, and some manufacturers say their units have such durable components that they can then be refurbished, fitted with new engines, and put back to work. It almost goes without saying that engine technology has progressed considerably too. Whether a new ADT is powered by a Caterpillar, Cummins, Detroit Diesel, Deutz, Mercedes, Scania, or Volvo engine, the latest trucks all offer similar gains in reliability, improved fuel consumption, reduced emissions, longer intervals between oil changes, and so on. These smart, electronically controlled diesels are hooked up to a central computer and linked to the electronics governing transmissions, allowing power delivery to the wheels to be optimized.

But there may be further developments to come with regard to ADT drivelines that could depart from relying on prop shafts and universal joints. Terex's Unit Rig subsidiary unveiled an innovative scraper prototype some years ago that featured a sophisticated new hydrostatic

drive capable of far higher travel speeds than were feasible before. In fact, the driveline was clearly suitable for use on an ADT as well. And while development of the prototype scraper was not taken further by Terex, the potential for a hydrostatic drive has yet to be fully explored on an ADT, as it offers considerable advantages in terms of drive on uneven surfaces and braking, despite its slightly lower operating efficiency, than a comparable mechanical drivetrain.

Size Matters

When ADTs first started to work on-site, payloads were small and ranged from the 17 U.S. tons/15 tonnes of Moxy's D15 to 22 U.S. tons/20 tonnes for the early Volvo models. It was DJB that pushed the boundaries of ADT capacity, with its twin-axle D25 and D30 models, rated at 25 U.S. tons/23 tonnes and 30 U.S. tons/27 tonnes respectively.

As the ADT market developed, the biggest volume segment soon became the 25-U.S.-ton/23-tonne-capacity class, and this held true for many years. But the ADT is still a comparatively recent machine development, and there has

Volvo's A70 was developed specially for Norwegian firm SNSK to carry coal over a glacier, but the risk posed by sudden blizzards prompted SNSK to build a tunnel housing a conveyor under the glacier instead.

been a major shift over the years with an increasing number of customers switching to 40-U.S.-ton/36-tonne-payload machines instead.

The DJB line was the first to offer a 40-U.S.-ton/36-tonne-class machine, and the company even developed a 50 tonner, the DJB 550. Because of its payload, the DJB/Cat D550's launch generated some interest, and DJB built over 100 of the units, which were supplied with both the DJB and Caterpillar names. Performance was not satisfactory, though, largely due to the fact that its engine wasn't powerful enough to cope with its relatively high unladen weight, as a result of which the machines were nowhere near as fast on grade as the smaller ADTs of the time. Looking at the specifications, it is clear how this shortfall occurred. DJB's D550 had a Cat engine rated at 450 horsepower/336 kilowatts and weighed 42 U.S. tons/37.8 tonnes unladen, while the later Caterpillar D550B model had a 460-horsepower/343-kilowatt diesel and weighed 45 U.S. tons/40.8 tonnes clean. By comparison, Cat's first D400 ADT weighed 28.6 U.S. tons/25.8 tonnes unladen, had a 40-U.S.-ton-s/36.3-tonne payload, and was driven by an engine rated at 385 horsepower/287 kilowatts (figures that are not so far behind current machines). Doing some simple arithmetic, the D400 had 6.87 horsepower/U.S. ton 4.62 kilowatts per tonne gross vehicle weight (GVW) it had to shift, while the D550 had 5.7 horsepower per U.S. ton/3.83 kilowatts per tonne of GVW, and the D550B had 5.65 horsepower per U.S. ton/3.8 kilowatts per tonne of GVW. Caterpillar certainly built more powerful engines, but squeezing them between the chassis rails and into the length of the available engine compartment was not feasible. A longer front chassis would have been needed, and this would have made the truck larger and heavier still, as well as making it more cumbersome. With axle problems also starting to occur as the machines clocked hours on-site, the decision was made to cut production of this model, though the main reason for the D550's failure was the low power-to-weight ratio.

Other attempts were being made to build bigger ADTs. In 1991, the Wagner Fullback 645 prototype was rolled out, and when it entered production it was as the upgraded Fullback 650, offering a 50-U.S.-ton/45.4-tonne capacity. The firm was bullish about this model and even considered a larger version with a capacity as high as 65

As with rigid trucks, most ADTs have a buddy seat, which comes in useful when a trainee is learning fine tips on machine control from a more experienced operator.

U.S. tons/60 tonnes that would rival rigid quarry trucks. But like the earlier DJB design, the Fullback simply did not have enough power under the hood, and the idea for an even larger model was shelved. It is worth noting that the Fullback used the same 12.7-liter Detroit Diesel 60 series engine (which has a good reputation in the industry) as the Terex 40-U.S.-ton/36-tonne-payload ADT of the period. Rated at 400 horsepower/298 kilowatts in the Terex 4066C of the mid-1990s, this was sufficient for a 40-U.S.-ton/36-tonne capacity truck. The engine delivered 450 horsepower/336 kilowatts in the heavier FB-650, which tipped the scales at nearly 40 U.S. tons/36 tonnes unladen. While the Wagner machine's lighter weight gave it a power-to-weight ratio that was slightly better than that of the earlier DJB/Cat D550, the Fullback was still regarded with skepticism in the industry. There were reports of transmission problems too, and though a few machines were used on-site, the FB-650 was dropped unceremoniously from Atlas Copco Wagner's range in the late 1990s.

In Belarus, the rigid-truck manufacturer MoAZ also rolled out a 55-U.S.-ton/50-tonne-payload truck called the 7503. With its side-mounted cab, this machine closely resembled the old DJB 550, and it is worth noting that two of the DJB machines were exported to Russia to work in a mining operation. However, the 7503 had its cab forward of the front axle, whereas the cab was on top of the front axle on the DJB 550. There was also a resemblance in the design of the dump body on the MoAZ machine to that of the DJB 550. The MoAZ 7503 was powered by a YaMZ engine delivering 600 horsepower/441 kilowatts, driving through a six-speed gearbox to four of the six wheels (DJB's 550 had a 6x4 drive—another similarity between the two). The performance of the 7503 matched that of other ADTs, according to the manufacturer, as the truck had a top speed of 30 miles per hour/50 kilometers per hour and a 41-cubic-yard/32-cubic-meter heaped capacity in its body. Tipping the scales at 42 U.S. tons/38 tonnes unladen, the machine offered a creditable power-to-weight ratio of 7.43 horsepower per ton/5 kilowatts per tonne when it was carrying a full load (though there was no information available concerning its driveline efficiency). How many of these units were built is not clear, and there

Different firms place the swivel for the rear-dump body in different locations, either forward or rearward of the articulation joint, with advantages claimed for both.

Above and right: There are huge variations in design and construction of dump bodies for ADTs, with some firms favoring relatively straight-sided units made largely from steel plate and others building more bowl-shaped units.

is little known about their performance in the dirt, as they were not exported outside of the CIS countries.

The most successful large ADT so far has come from Bell. Although the B50 has a smaller payload than the DJB 550, the Wagner Fullback 650, or the MoAZ 7503, there are several fleets of the Bell machines now in use. The first step in the development of the B50 was the B45 prototype, a 45-U.S.-ton/41-tonne-capacity machine that was basically a stretched B40 intended to test the concept. This truck featured the air-cooled disc brakes of the B40 model current at that time, though the firm knew right from the start that the larger payload of the B50 would require oil-immersed brakes.

Bell has been able to use its extensive ADT experience to position its machine in the market more carefully than the earlier DJB/Cat and Atlas Copco Wagner machines. And Bell has also been able to take advantage of numerous technical advances. Current diesels are more compact, more fuel-efficient, more powerful, and cleaner running than before. When the Atlas Copco Wagner truck was available, the firm was keen to push the machine into earthmoving but never succeeded in developing a market. This was not helped by the facts that the firm had been out of the surface equipment sector for many years and the Fullback 650 was the only ADT model Wagner produced.

Coming at a time when the off-highway equipment market was experiencing an undeniable slowdown in sales, Bell's introduction of a full-production 50-U.S.-ton/45-tonne ADT was significant. Launching the product was a calculated gamble, which required significant investment

in research and development during the seven years of prototype testing. And Bell's B50 ADT differed from the earlier DJB and MoAZ machines in that it offered a true 6x6 driveline. Power for the first version of the B50 was supplied by a V-8 Mercedes-Benz diesel rated at up to 470 horsepower/350 kilowatts, fitted with electronic controls.

Designed with the mining industry in mind, the B50 payload was carried in a 36-cubic-yard/28.2-cubic-meter rock body, supported on a specially developed, heavy-duty rear chassis. Although many of the technical advances used in the B50 came from improved components, the firm had to pay special attention to a number of key areas during the truck's development. Keeping a close eye on weight and driveline design were crucial for the Bell engineering team.

Most of the components needed for the B50 came onto the market at around the same time. The necessary high-power-density engine, improved planetary transmission, and associated final driveline hardware, along with logic-based control systems, were all crucial for the B50. These components and technologies were necessary for a truck of this size, with the final key being announcements from both Goodyear and Michelin of new high-flotation tires developed specifically for the needs of the ADT market. The tires were important as they allowed increased axle loads in poor underfoot conditions. The first pre-production B50 made its public debut at the 2002 Electra Mining Show in Johannesburg.

Bell's smaller-capacity trucks had Mercedes OM 906-series engines combined with ZF model transmissions,

115

When Terex dropped its distinctive green color scheme for its trucks, the firm changed to white and grey, explaining that this offered high visibility on-site and improved safety.

with Mercedes OM 501 series V-6-configuration engines and Allison transmissions specified for the larger machines. It was no surprise that Bell's engineers considered a Mercedes engine for the B50 (though other diesels were evaluated), opting for the OM 500 series as it offered the power density and low fuel-burn characteristics required. A 15.9-liter 502LA V-8, as used in the heavy-duty Mercedes-Benz road trucks, was selected, but as this was some 300 millimeters longer than the V-6 501, Bell had to stretch the front chassis. At the same time, the cab profile had to be raised by 100 millimeters to maintain the operator's field of view over the engine cover.

To achieve the payload target Bell was aiming for with its B50, the choice of engine was crucial to deliver the right power-to-weight ratio, and the 500 series diesels came with several improvements suitable for ADTs. In spite of the additional power and torque, though, the 502 engine was still fuel efficient, with low exhaust emissions too.

The top-of-the-range, big-block 502LA developed 510 horsepower/380 kilowatts at 1,800 rpm. Given the B50's GVW of 89 U.S. tons/80 tonnes, the power-to-weight ratio was 7.06 horsepower per U.S. ton /4.75 kilowatts per tonne GVW, a considerable gain over the 5.65 horsepower per ton/3.8 kilowatts per tonne of DJB's D550B and on par with conventional 40-U.S.-ton/36-tonne payload trucks from several manufacturers. Moreover, this power output was conservative, as the 502LA could be rated at up to 600 horsepower/448 kilowatts.

The engine was mated to a six-speed, close-ratio planetary transmission with electronic controls, allowing adjustments to any shift instruction to suit speed, load, and conditions, as well as featuring maintenance and diagnostic tools. An early lock-up from second gear up, combined with narrower ratio splits, gave good acceleration and better response. This lock-up helped improve mechanical efficiency due to the closely spaced gear steps, while the system had two overdrive ratios as well. The system was said to allow progressive shifting techniques, minimizing engine speed for a lower fuel burn.

Another key issue for the B50 was the integration of its electronic controls, with its engine management system able to communicate with transmission and hydraulic controls. This allowed the ABS, engine retarder, and transmission system to be integrated with the management module in the cab. To provide an even spread of power and good travel speeds required a two-speed reduction capability, and although Bell had fitted early 40-U.S.-ton/36-tonne-capacity trucks with remote-mounted, manually operated two-speed Steyr transfer cases, these had limitations. The trucks had to be stationary for shifting, and the function couldn't be automated, so benefits to speed and fuel consumption would be lost if the operator forgot to use the system, which would also have been heavy. Bell's solution was to select a conventional VGR interaxle with proportional differential, combined with two-speed differentials. This layout offered good gradeability and top speed.

To allow the increased payload, minimizing the unladen weight of the B50 was as important as installing a powerful engine. One way this was achieved was by using the firm's fabricated axle design, rather than using heavier castings. Bell's experience making fabricated axles had allowed it to develop high-grade units that it reckoned were as strong as cast components, yet were 25 to 30 percent lighter. The structure of the Bell truck's chassis also relied on these precision-made, fabricated components, rather than having castings and forgings as used by other manufacturers in their more conventionally sized trucks.

However, major investment had to be made in material selection and quality control to make this work. All ADT builders use alloy steels for dump bodies and chassis, but Bell had to take special care with its B50 to maximize structural strength and minimize weight. Even when fitted with a full body-liner package for use in hard-rock mining, the unladen weight of the B50 was under 37 U.S. tons/34 tonnes. Bell's engineers achieved this by selecting steel with good formability and welding properties. The firm used

Large sites can require large fleets, and this mine reinstatement operation in Germany used large numbers of ADTs for areas where ground conditions were soft.

On a wet and curving descent, an ADT of any make offers safer operation than a rigid truck due to the all-wheel drive, as well as the various transmission controls intended to reduce slip.

steels with yield strengths of 300 MPa in nonstructural components and 700 MPa steels for the chassis and body.

Because of the extra payload, it was clear from the start that the B50 would require more powerful brakes than before. Although in normal operating conditions engine exhaust braking and transmission retardation is used to slow a truck down, effective brakes also have to be installed to ensure maximum safety in all conditions. During the development of the B50, the prototype B45 had used the same dry discs at the rear as seen on the then-current B40 model, and Bell's engineers knew that this braking system would be insufficient for the safety requirements of a production model.

The firm had developed an enclosed braking system for its B40 with full hydraulic oil–immersed brakes on the front and second axle that paved the way for the system used in the B50, which used wet-plate braking on all three axles. The system was developed by Bell's R&D engineering group and had a sophisticated design intended to provide high braking capabilities while also being easy to maintain with minimum downtime.

The majority of oil-immersed, multiplate systems utilize several external pumps, valves, and oil reservoirs, all linked through connections between the axles, as well as large remote-mounted heat exchangers equipped with thermal controls. But Bell developed a simple, self-contained system that didn't need to have external oil routing or components for extra cooling. Bell also broke with convention by using aluminum alloy castings for the wheel hubs housing the friction-plate assembly. Although costly to manufacture, this offered efficient oil flow through the fabricated axles, which themselves acted as heat exchangers and eliminated the need for additional cooling. Bell carried out extensive testing during the development of the B50, and the system showed it could keep oil temperatures easily within the limits required, even in hard braking.

A further feature of the B50 that was relatively new to the ADT sector (but well accepted for rigid trucks) was the installation of an onboard payload weighing system. The system was fitted primarily to prevent overloading, and it fed the data to the truck's vehicle information system using an array of strain gauges and filters fitted at key

For sites featuring steep-ramp hauls, the ADT is the only production hauler that can be relied on to carry a full load without its wheels losing traction, even in the wet.

points around the machine. However, it also enabled the truck user to have access to production information in real time, allowing detailed analysis of the cost per ton in a given operation. All in all, Bell was sure the extra payload of the B50 gave it an edge over conventional ADTs, allowing it to compete against larger rigid trucks as well. While rigid trucks have operating advantages in terms of comparative mechanical simplicity that makes them easy to maintain, the rear-wheel-drive configuration restricts their operation to well drained and maintained haul roads with relatively shallow gradients. And though the Terex/Payhauler 4WD rigid truck offered larger capacity and good traction, it was a niche product and only sold in relatively small numbers. By comparison, Bell's B50 is able to carry on running even in soft, wet conditions or steep-ramp hauls, as well as at high speeds on an open haul road. A key point in Bell's decision to develop the B50 was that the machine would appeal strongly to the rental market, as its higher capacity and operational versatility would ensure far higher utilization than could be achieved with a rigid truck with a similar payload. And like Atlas Copco Wagner with

its Fullback 650, Bell is convinced that there is still a potential for a larger-capacity ADT.

It is worth remembering, though, that the 50-U.S.-ton/45-tonne-capacity B50 is not the biggest ADT to reach series production. The Wagner Fullback 650 offered 45-U.S.-ton/50-tonne payloads, while the DJB 550 and MoAZ 7503 had capacities of 55 U.S. tons/50 tonnes. And even these three are outclassed in terms of payload by Volvo's A70, with its 70-U.S.-ton/65-tonne capacity.

The Volvo A70 was a special machine designed and built to a special request for a special application, and the firm manufactured a small fleet for the Norwegian coal producer SNSK. Based on Volvo's A40, the A70 used the same front suspension, chassis, cab, engine, and transmission, but with a longer rear chassis mounted on three axles (instead of the usual two), which made it capable of taking a bigger body. Because of this configuration, the A70 didn't score highly in terms of its power-to-weight ratio, but this was not an issue, due to the nature of the application. In fact, the machine provided reliable duty for SNSK. The coal mine where this truck fleet ran is located on the Norwegian archipelago of Spitsbergen, south of the northern polar ice cap. The mine entrance lies just above a glacier, and the trucks were required to run laden downhill, which is why the power-to-weight ratio wasn't critical, though the braking systems did have to be very effective. The haul road was particularly unusual, lying as it did on top of the glacier and running to the coal terminal by the port. And this is the only semi-permanent ice road in the world, as all other ice roads are seasonal and can only be negotiated in the winter. SNSK was keen on an ADT because it wanted an all-wheel-drive machine able to negotiate the ice road in the sometimes extremely harsh winter conditions so as to maximize traction and safety. As existing ADTs did not have sufficient payload and because the laden haul was downhill, SNSK and Volvo came up with the special A70 configuration to meet this unusual requirement. When SNSK decided to increase mine output and efficiency further and to increase safety levels because of concerns over running the trucks—whiteouts due to sudden blizzards are not unknown in these conditions—the firm built a tunnel under the glacier with a conveyor belt. This lessened the need for the special A70s, though the machines had operated reliably in this extremely difficult application for a number of years.

Manufacturers have considered building ADTs bigger than the A70, though these have never passed the basic design sketch stage. In the late 1970s and early 1980s, U.K. ADT pioneer DJB sketched some designs for a truck with a payload as high as 200 U.S. tons/180 tonnes. The DJB machine would have featured twin engines and drivelines, utilizing the diesels and transmissions from Cat's 777 rigid truck, which had been introduced a few years earlier. But with the technology available at the time, the DJB design was considered a step too far and the concept was shelved.

Underground Too

Some contractors and mining firms are keen on using modified surface trucks for underground operations, and ADTs are often specified for this purpose. Bell in particular, as well as Volvo, has had success in this sector, with numerous fleets of three-axle machines operating in Australia and Latin America. Terex also converted a number of machines for these applications, with machines running in Australia and Germany.

The Bell, Terex, and Volvo ADTs adapted for use underground share similar modifications. Most are fitted with special electronics to meet underground mining regulations, cut-down cabs and headboards to lower overall height, and catalytic converters to reduce engine emissions. Additional lighting is usually fitted on the cab for forward visibility as well as on the body itself, so that the drivers

can make sure that the load is not so high that it brushes against the roof of the mine and spills onto the roadway. Also, to improve visibility underground, closed-circuit television (CCTV) equipment is sometimes fitted to help when reversing. Other equipment includes radio systems and fire-suppression kits to meet underground mining regulations.

However, Volvo's four-wheel-drive, short-wheelbase A25 is an anomaly in the market, as it is the only ADT that is purpose-built for mining and tunneling. The machine comes with Volvo's novel hydraulically lowering wheels as an option, allowing the vehicle to turn around in confined areas. By dropping wheels into position, the rear of the machine lifts and the truck can turn 180 degrees in a tunnel just 31.2 feet/9.5 meters wide. Payload is 27 U.S. tons/24 tonnes and capacity is 16.6 cubic yards/13 cubic meters for the purpose-built body, while the truck offers a travel speed of 33 miles per hour/53 kilometers per hour. Power comes from a six-cylinder Volvo diesel, delivering 306 horsepower/228 kilowatts, and standard driveline features include exhaust and hydraulic transmission retarders. The drivetrain has a torque converter with automatic lock-up, six-speed transmission, a single-stage drop box, differential locks, and hydraulic retarder. Braking is by dual-circuit dry discs, and the truck is also equipped with Volvo's load-and-dump brake system.

Nose Ahead

One of the visible changes that has occurred with ADTs in recent years has been at the front end. Visually, most of the new trucks on the market bear the rounded Roman noses and wraparound cab glass that have become all the rage since Moxy unveiled its MT36 some years ago. One-piece, lightweight engine covers made of glass-reinforced plastic (GRP) are now commonplace, combined with the wraparound glass that affords an operator better forward visibility. These machines contrast strongly with early ADTs from Volvo that showed signs of their roots in agricultural tractors or from the scraper-influenced designs of DJB/Caterpillar with their side-mounted cabs.

Nowadays, Bell, Caterpillar, CNH/Linkbelt, Hydrema, JCB, Moxy, Terex, and Volvo all have ADTs with sloping engine covers that allow the operator to see much closer to the front end of the machine. This is a key issue, given the way ADTs are used, and considering the sloping-ramp hauls they may have to operate on. Cresting a steep climb with the front end pointing at an angle upward, it is extremely difficult to see forward.

It was Norwegian firm Moxy that broke the pattern set earlier by Volvo, which had stemmed from the agricultural tractors on which its first ADT designs were based.

Moxy was first to develop an ADT with a wrap-around windscreen and sloping engine cover on its MT36, with the design then being introduced to other models in the lineup.

The square-edged cab and front end of the older-generation ADTs gave way to the new Moxy MT36 prototype that premiered at the Intermat construction equipment exhibition in Paris in 1997.

This machine won design awards for its new approach to ADT cab layout, with a raft of new ideas never tried on these machines before. The trend-setting MT36 offered a wide and curved windscreen, following the lead set many years before in the automotive sector and standing well apart from the flat windscreens of rival ADTs of the period. Moreover, the Moxy designers had taken full advantage of the relatively small block of Scania diesels powering the truck by sloping the engine cover and mounting the radiator lower in the front chassis member. Understandably, the MT36 attracted a great deal of attention from rival firms, and although Moxy did not put the MT36 into production for some time after the prototype made its appearance, the die had been cast. As successive model upgrades came from rivals Bell, Caterpillar, CNH/Linkbelt, Terex, and Volvo (as well as Hydrema and JCB at the lower end of the payload scale), these competing firms all introduced ADTs with sloping engine covers.

However, just because the engine covers of the newer generation of ADTs slope, this did not mean competing firms had followed every feature of Moxy's MT36. In this respect, the Caterpillar trucks are the most distinctive, as the radiator and oil-cooling systems are all mounted behind the cab rather than in front of the engine as is commonplace. And although Volvo has not taken such a radical step, it uses split radiators that are mounted on

either side and have fans pushing hot air out, rather than drawing cool air in. This layout reduces the amount of dirt in the engine compartment, and Volvo says it is just as effective at cooling as the more conventional method of drawing the air into the engine. According to Volvo, when an ADT is operating, there is little benefit with a conventional cooling layout with air rushing into the engine compartment. These machines are generally only moving at 15 to 20 miles per hour/24 to 32 kilometers per hour in the majority of applications, so the forced-air cooling effect is minimal. Moving the radiator to the rear of the cab does require longer hoses, while having a split radiator requires more pipework. However, both Caterpillar and Volvo say the engine cooling offered by their current trucks is every bit as effective and there are benefits in terms of maintenance access. Like Moxy, though, Bell, CNH/Linkbelt, and Terex have been able to benefit from using engines with comparatively compact blocks and have been able to keep a single radiator at the front without compromising engine-cooling efficiency.

It is worth noting, though, that having a radiator anywhere other than in front of the engine is by no means a new innovation. Early cars from French manufacturer Renault were distinctive, as the radiators were mounted behind the engines, a configuration later used by Mack on its famous AC and AP trucks. The Mack trucks had good forward visibility for their time, due to their sloping engine covers, and they were extremely rugged in design and manufacture, so many of them ended up hauling dirt on mining and construction projects. It is not clear why none of the ADT builders have chosen this option, as modern airflow technology could eliminate any cab-heating effects experienced with the old Renault cars or Mack trucks. It would also be feasible to achieve a low-profile hood/bonnet design for an ADT using an air-cooled engine, but the current direction of exhaust legislation rules this out. Air-cooled engines may not be able to meet coming emissions targets and also have serious cab-heating issues, as the early Terex ADTs showed.

But it is worth noting that other manufacturers had not followed the lead set originally by Volvo. For many years, the larger Caterpillar/DJB ADTs with payloads of 35 U.S. tons/32 tonnes and 40 U.S. tons/36 tonnes all featured an offset cab design akin to that seen on the front end of a scraper. David Brown's thinking on this feature had long been that the offset cab allowed for a shorter front chassis, given that the Cat engines of the time had slightly larger blocks than some of their competitors. The layout also afforded better forward visibility and gave a good rear view when reversing up to a wheel loader, excavator, or dump area. Other reasons for this configuration were that the side-mounted cab allowed a lower center of gravity that boosted front-end stability, while also reducing the height of the seating position for the driver and making for less of a swaying motion when traversing uneven ground. Brown commented that as it worked well enough on a scraper, there was no harm in using it on an ADT too. DJB and Caterpillar persisted with this layout for the 35-U.S.-ton/32-tonne and 40-U.S.-ton/36-tonne trucks until 2001, when the radically different 735 and 740 were unveiled.

In this regard, though, the Cat/DJB machines differed from all the competitors (with the exception of MoAZ), such as Bell, Moxy, Terex, and Volvo, which placed the cab more or less centrally. The cab offset was less pronounced on the smaller Cat/DJB ADTs, and while a slight offset could also be seen in the cabs of the Terex 4066 and later TA40, this last was due to the location of the hydraulic systems.

There are numerous pros and cons regarding cab location for ADTs, and the larger Caterpillar machines persisted with the side-mounted design for many years, though the firm now builds machines with centrally mounted cabs instead. The thinking behind having a centrally mounted cab is that this offers better ride quality, as the driver's seat effectively rotates about a point if a

Fully loading an ADT results in higher productivity, as with any type of haul machine, but care must be taken to minimize spillage, as this necessitates further clearing up and burns additional fuel.

Terex's series 7 ADTs sported the sloping engine cover design to maximize forward visibility, as well as a host of driveline upgrades to increase performance. *Ettore Zanatta*

front wheel drops into a hole. In comparison, a truck with a side-mounted cab will give the operator an up-and-down motion when it is crossing undulating terrain. Manufacturers building trucks with centrally mounted cabs all agree that this configuration reduces the effects of pitch and roll and minimizes front-to-back movement for the driver, and this leads to higher comfort and better productivity.

The benefits are not just limited to ride comfort. With a centrally mounted cab, the driver tends to have a higher seating position, which helps give good overall visibility and a high field of sight.

Even so, it is not correct to say that a centrally located cab gives the best field of vision in all instances, and the old Cat trucks had side-mounted cabs for a good reason. DJB designed them that way because the layout had shown itself very effective on scrapers and gave a good view down one side, which came in useful when reversing to a dump point or to an excavator or wheel loader for loading purposes. The DJB/Cat ADTs also had side-mounted cabs, as this was one way to keep the front chassis short and afford a good forward view over the front end of the machine. This was particularly important at the time

when the DJB/Cat ADTs were first designed, as engine blocks were larger than at present.

Like cab design and placement, ADT suspension systems have advanced considerably, though not always in the same direction. Some new ADTs are fitted with novel self-leveling systems using computers to track the speed of the truck, weight, and angle of articulation that then send a signal to adjust the suspension strut. Not every firm uses the same suspension layout, though, and this is particularly evident at the front end of an ADT. Many manufacturers fit strut-type suspensions, as these are relatively simple, durable, and give good travel. However, Hydrema, fits its 922 with a strut-and-beam axle layout that is controlled electronically to improve ride quality. By comparison, Komatsu fits a DeDion-type front suspension, Terex uses a leading-arm/cross-tube configuration at the front, and on some Volvo machines the front axle is suspended at three points with twin shock absorbers.

Body Talk

For many years, manufacturers have followed different paths when it comes to dump-body design, though the dividing lines of the past have been eroded. Broadly speaking, the ADT builders separated into two camps: those making trucks with flat-sided bodies and those preferring a sloping design. Caterpillar, Terex, and Volvo all started making trucks with flat-sided bodies some years ago, using thick and durable Hardox plating for stiffness and good wear properties. These featured the familiar V-shaped profile when seen from the end, and although the three firms had their own designs, they all followed similar principles. Additional stiffening was provided by the top edge and floor of the body, with pivot points welded in place on either side for the hoist rams. The bodies all sat on top of flat rear chassis, again following broadly similar principles in terms of structure (though the rear suspensions varied considerably).

In marked contrast, Bell and Moxy had opted for the sloping design, still with a V-shaped profile, with thinner plating and vertical stiffeners to add strength. These bodies sat on top of a sloping rear chassis that angled downwards from the rear axles toward the articulation joint. Bell maintains that the sloping chassis and deep-bowl body configuration provide better stability in uneven ground, adding that this does not affect material ejection. Terex had also offered a similar design on its first-generation ADTs, though this was replaced with a flat rear chassis, as already seen on the Cat and Volvo machines when Terex's B series appeared in the early 1990s.

All the firms had their reasons to believe their body designs were the best. Caterpillar, Terex, and Volvo agreed that the flat body was comparatively simple to manufacture, rugged, durable, and allowed for good weight distribution across the rear axles carrying most of the payload. All three firms agreed that a flatter chassis allows them to build a relatively simple dump body that is strong and rugged and that will eject material effectively without having a negative effect on stability. Volvo says that a thick plate design only requires extra plating in the very toughest applications. This design is less likely to bulge out with use, which in turn can cause material retention during tipping, and Volvo added that a straight-sided dump body can also be loaded with a wheel loader more easily.

Meanwhile, Bell and Moxy said that using thinner plating with stiffeners allowed for a lighter body that could carry slightly more payload, yet was every bit as strong and durable. Moreover, Bell and Moxy claimed that the slope of the body floor allowed better material retention (and less spillage), a lower center of gravity that improved stability, and better weight distribution across the whole truck.

But while tipping bodies dominate the ADT market in terms of sales, ejector trucks have brought a new dimension to the sector. The appearance of the DDT ejector concept in the mid-1990s fired the imaginations of

engineers at other firms, and several models subsequently came on the market. Whatever the technical shortcomings of the original DDT design, the concept had undeniable merit and offered benefits in terms of safety and material spreading. As DDT had claimed from the start, the ejector body offered distinct advantages in terms of being able to dump a load safely on uneven ground or on a slope, even at right angles to the slope if necessary, without risk of rolling over. Moreover, the ejector truck could be relied upon to dump sticky materials such as wet clay, without any carryback that would reduce operating efficiency by reducing the truck's payload.

U.S. truck body specialist Phillippi-Hagenbuch has built a number of ejector truck bodies, mainly for use on landfill sites for spreading waste that were fitted to Volvo chassis and more recently onto Komatsu ADTs. Caterpillar engineer Peter Prillinger also developed an ejector body for the firm's then-top-of-the-line D400E using a good deal of proven ejector componentry sourced from the firm's scrapers. And Bell unveiled a novel ejector body soon after that used heavy-duty steel chains instead of a hydraulic ram to haul the headboard back.

Of these, the Phillippi-Hagenbuch ejector bodies are sold in limited volumes but are reasonably successful in a small niche market. By comparison, the Bell ejector body was not a success and has since disappeared from the market. However, it is Caterpillar that has sold the largest number of ejector-type ADTs by far. The firm's ejector truck had its origins in a few older D400 models that were converted to this format by an enterprising contractor in the United States. The contractor had initially tried the DDT machines but found them wanting and decided it could build a better version using the D400 as a basis. These units were relatively simple but gave good service, and Caterpillar itself soon became very interested, working closely with the contractor to develop an improved design. The ADT ejector mechanism Caterpillar developed wasn't simple, but it was well engineered and, as it used proven ejector-bowl components from the firm's scrapers, it worked well without experiencing the jamming that had occurred with the DDT in cold weather.

This still wasn't perfect, though, and the original model was criticized as its body was heavier than a standard tipping body, reducing payload by around 0.55 U.S. tons/0.5 tonnes. But with further refinements Caterpillar was able to minimize the weight penalty while further increasing the reliability and durability of the ejector mechanism. It took a while before Cat's ejector system was taken seriously, but when the company replaced its 40-U.S.-ton/36-tonne-capacity D400EII truck with the 740, an ejector was again offered. Like the earlier truck, this machine was able to dump material as it moved and was suited to duties in low-height areas such as tunneling applications or sites with overhead powerlines. The 740 Ejector is also able to operate in ultra-soft ground areas, such as those found on mine reclamation jobs or waste handling, more easily than a conventional ADT. With the 740's improved body design, load capacity was increased to 42 U.S. tons/38 tonnes, and this was one of a number of improvements. The electronically controlled 3406E ATAAC engine met the latest exhaust-emission regulations and was rated at 415 horsepower/309.5 kilowatts, while the electronically controlled, seven-speed transmission was based on the proven system fitted to the 769 rigid truck. The 740 Ejector truck had other new features, including a box section front chassis, revised suspension system, upgraded hitch, and of course, Cat's center-mounted cab with rear-fitted radiator. Caterpillar later expanded its ejector-truck line with a smaller version, based on its 30-U.S.-ton/27-tonne-capacity 730 as well. Numerous fleets of the Caterpillar ejector machines are now in use in duties ranging from waste handling to road construction. Although ejector ADTs suit a niche market, they have steady sales.

There has been one other contender in the ejector-truck market, and although it is not strictly an ADT, the Multidrive M8-40 should not be overlooked. Also a product of David Brown's ingenuity, the M8-40 offered a different kind of competition altogether. This unusual vehicle came with an ejector body and bridged the gap between a conventional on/off-highway tipper truck and the ADT, with a number of features and performance characteristics from both. The M8-40 model came with a 40-U.S.-ton /36-tonne payload and a 51-cubic-yard/40-cubic-meter-capacity in a truck with a similar operating envelope to a 25-U.S.-ton/23-tonne-class ADT, according to Mr. Brown. With its four axles and 8WD, the M8-40 had even weight distribution and cycle times that were up to 37 percent faster than conventional ADTs. This truck was aimed at applications such as coal hauling or reinstatement of sites with poor underfoot conditions and offered additional benefits in terms of reduced tire wear, costs, and roadway maintenance.

One of the key features of the M8-40 was its low unladen weight of just 24 U.S. tons/22 tonnes, which

Volvo developed a version of its A25D with twin axles, a shortened rear chassis, and a special body for use in applications such as tunnelling. Options included special wheels at the rear that could be lowered hydraulically and could lift up the rear end of the truck, turning it around where space was tight. *Volvo collection*

made it fully road legal in many countries. With power coming from a 450-horsepower/336-kilowatt Cat diesel driving through a six-speed, two-range Allison automatic transmission, the truck had a top speed of 56 miles per hour/89.6 kilometers per hour on the flat and could climb grades up to 60 percent when fully laden. The firm said its M8-40 offered increased speed, stability, and fuel efficiency over rough terrain when compared with ADTs. And Multidrive added that the M8-40 also provided big fuel savings—up to 60 percent when compared to a conventional dump truck—delivering the lowest cost per ton.

Material ejection was achieved using a patented, heavy-duty conveyor belt that could dump a full load in 15 seconds. In addition, the truck driver could control the ejection rate, either heaping or spreading the load as the vehicle was traveling. The company said the conveyor/headboard system eliminated carryback and allowed a lighter material to be used in the body, reducing operating weight. The cab resembled those fitted to on-highway vehicles, giving the M8-40 plenty of room for two people, while the firm reckoned the truck's sophisticated suspension system offered a ride superior to that of any machine in the ADT sector.

Stop and Go

Making sure a truck is able to stop when required is every bit as important as getting it to move under its own power, and there has been a huge leap forward in terms of braking and retardation technology. The first ADTs were equipped with drum brakes, and these suffered all the expected problems expected, such as brake fade under hard use and the need for regular brake shoe replacement. Drum brakes are also subject to problems stemming from severe overheating, which can require the drums to be replaced. This can be expensive and time consuming, further adding to costs.

Clearly a better braking solution was required, and manufacturers soon found that the disc brakes by that time becoming widespread in the automotive sector were well suited to use on ADTs despite the much lower travel speeds involved.

For many years now, air-cooled disc brakes have been used successfully on ADTs, and these are still fitted to the smaller 25–30-U.S.-ton/23–27-tonne trucks as a rule. But air-cooled discs, though comparatively simple and well proven, also have their shortcomings. In dusty conditions or in applications with fine-grit particles, dry disc-brake systems can be subject to high wear levels and may require regular maintenance. Dry discs can also overheat, and if the problem is allowed to persist, the discs can become distorted and require replacement, at no small cost and resulting in additional downtime and reduced site productivity.

As a result, many of the ADTs in the 35–40-U.S.-ton/32–36-tonne class now have more complex oil-immersed brake systems (and these are also fitted to Bell's B50, as mentioned earlier). Oil-immersed brakes are used on the larger trucks because these machines have bigger payloads to carry and have a greater need for the additional retardation. As the bigger trucks are more expensive in any case, the higher cost of the wet-plate disc brake systems is also better absorbed into the total purchase price. Some of these trucks have the wet-plate discs on two axles, while others have more sophisticated systems operating on all three, but in general these offer superior performance and lower maintenance requirements. The truck manufacturers have managed to provide effective hydraulic cooling for the wet-plate systems (sometimes using novel methods, as seen on Bell's B50). This has been no small step, given that cooling is often carried out forward of the articulation joint and that the hydraulic fluid has to be carried past this point to link with the rear axle or axles fitted with the wet-plate discs.

However, ADTs do not rely solely on disc brakes to stop. Further retardation is also given by exhaust brakes, while hydraulic retarders are fitted as standard on many machines with payloads of 30 U.S. tons/27 tonnes or more. These latter systems are often options on the 25-U.S.-ton/23-tonne trucks that still dominate the ADT sales figures.

Another small but important improvement in recent years is that hydraulic-brake actuation has now largely replaced the older air systems seen on early generations of ADTs. This is an important point, as air-controlled systems are vulnerable to freezing in cold weather, and given that ADTs are expected to run year round in many instances, this offers major safety benefits too.

Chapter 6
ON TRACK
ADTS GIVE BIRTH TO NEW MACHINES

South African company Bell made its first forays into the equipment sector with a three-wheeled utility machine that is still popular in its home market, but the firm is best known internationally for its articulated dump truck range. Bell's articulated dump trucks (ADTs) started rolling out of the factory in Richards Bay in 1986 and began making a serious play for a share of the worldwide market in the mid-1990s. However, the firm has made other interesting forays into the equipment sector, most noticeably with its recent development of a line of tractor units designed to tow scraper boxes. What makes this departure both interesting and slightly ironic is that the motor-scraper market has declined over the years, due in part to the success of Bell's mainstay, the ADT.

The ADT began to take hold of the earthmoving market during the 1970s and 1980s, initially in Scandinavia and the United Kingdom, and then spreading further afield, while sales of motor scrapers plunged. The once-common scraper has now become something of a rarity on-site, with relatively few fleets purchased in recent times. The problem is that while the motor scraper is an extremely efficient way of moving dirt in the right application, these machines are expensive to buy and run and

have limited versatility. Towed scrapers had been nudged to one side by the development of the faster and more productive motor scraper. While the market for towed scrapers had never gone away, these had become niche units sold in small volumes only. By comparison, the less-efficient combination of ADT and hydraulic excavator allows a far greater versatility, while also proving cheaper to buy and run.

To add to the irony, when Bell developed its heavy-duty tractor, it used the front end of its proven B40 articulated truck as the basis for the machine. The firm's first prototype was built around a Bell B40C, and this was used to evaluate the concept, with extensive tests carried out in South Africa in an array of different operating conditions and applications. It was at the Conexpo 2002 construction equipment exhibition in Las Vegas that Bell lifted the lid on this machine, unveiling its pre-production 4WD tractor unit partnered with a heavy-duty Miskin-towed scraper box that had been designed for just this purpose. This equipment combo soon began to claim sales, first in Bell's home market and then in North America. Bell's explanation for the success was that its tractor was able to breathe new life into the old concept of the towed scraper box.

Above and Left: Although the current Bell tractor was developed from an ADT, the firm has made rugged tractors for industrial applications in the past that even paved the way for the firm's present ADTs. *Bell collection*

The market for towed scrapers was never eliminated entirely, though most units were relatively lightly built and aimed at the agricultural sector. All the same, a small trickle of units was being used in construction and mining applications, and Bell spotted this and identified it as a potential business opportunity. Bell realized a rugged and durable machine would meet the market needs for a niche product and that by using proven ADT components, it could develop a tractor quickly and relatively inexpensively. By the time of Conexpo's 2002 show, the prototype units had already racked up considerable operating hours, allowing the firm to fine-tune its design. The pre-production unit also benefited from using components from the firm's latest B40D truck model. The machine attracted considerable interest, and Bell was convinced it had a saleable product that was nearly ready for market. Since that time, Bell has managed to carve out a niche for this efficient and versatile, yet comparatively low-cost tool.

Called the 4206, Bell's first tractor represented a step back to the future for that company. In the past, heavy-duty wheeled tractors had been manufactured by firms like Caterpillar and Euclid, and these units were used extensively in construction and mining operations, mainly to tow scraper boxes. But as equipment trends changed in the 1950s, these units began to be replaced, in most instances by larger and more sophisticated motorized scrapers. Given this history, it is important to recognize why both motor scrapers and towed scrapers rose in importance and then dwindled in more recent times.

During the 1960s and 1970s, major road building programs in the United States and Europe made the self-propelled scraper king of the dirt, with a huge selection of models available from a vast array of manufacturers. These were good days for firms building both towed and motor scrapers, causing something of a gold rush in the sector. However, the ensuing rapid rise in fleet numbers brought problems. An increase in the number of earthworks contracts led to more and more firms deciding to enter the business. But this had the knock-on effect of reducing prices, as competition for tenders became more acute. And when the number of contracts being put out to tender for large earthmoving jobs began to dry up, this had a dramatic effect on demand for self-propelled scrapers. In a sense, they disappeared like the dinosaurs because they were too specialized and too costly.

Bell points out that its tractor has many special features not seen on its ADTs, such as reconfigured gear ratios and driveline controls and a heavily beefed-up articulation joint to cope with the additional stresses of towing. *Bell collection*

In recent years, several new towed scraper boxes designed for rugged-site applications have become available from firms like Miskin and Reynolds, with Terex now amongst the contenders in this market as well.

With demand for motor scrapers plummeting, the array of machines being manufactured shrank drastically. Although in the 1970s there was a vast range of motorized scrapers made by the likes of Allis-Chalmers, Euclid, Fiat-Allis, International, John Deere, LeTourneau, WABCO, and Woolridge/Curtiss-Wright, these are all long out of production. At present, Terex and Caterpillar are the only manufacturers still making self-propelled scrapers for the world market (Terex's Chinese subsidiary North Hauler makes them for the Chinese market), with only a few small firms building limited numbers of machines. While Cat and Terex continue to upgrade their designs from time to time, these machines are no longer big sellers, and both manufacturers concentrate most of their attention on other product types, with the ADT having become a far more important machine for both companies. All the same, the dedicated scraper does still find a market, and according to Caterpillar, its latest models offer better productivity and lower operating costs than before, while Terex has also been updating its scraper line. Both firms offer new models with better operator stations, larger scraper bowls,

and sophisticated electronic monitoring systems to simplify maintenance. The scraper engines are governed by electronics that are integrated with the control systems for the automatic planetary powershift transmissions, allowing maximum power to the cutting edge and a high haul speed.

Old-style motor scraper fleets are a rare sight these days. To offer the greatest efficiency on large earthmoving jobs, they are best run in teams of four or five machines, which often includes a large dozer for pushfilling. As each scraper is costly, there is a large capital outlay in building such a fleet—dozers aren't cheap to run, either. Maintenance costs for motor scraper fleets cannot be ignored, as the machines are hard on drivelines and tires, while the necessary push dozers require regular undercarriage servicing. Motor scrapers are best suited to long-term earthwork with short hauls, as well as good weather and underfoot conditions. In effect, these machines are ideal for work on large projects such as new highway construction jobs, but there are few such contracts these days.

Even though self-propelled scrapers are costly to buy and run, they can still have a place on a modern construction or mining operation. For earthmoving work involving distances of less than 0.6 mile/1 kilometer, the scraper is still recognized as the most cost-efficient and effective solution. And, unlike an ADT, a scraper does not need to be loaded by another machine, so it can operate by itself as long as the conditions are not too difficult. By comparison, if an excavator used to load an ADT fleet breaks down, the entire operation will stop until repairs are made or a replacement excavator is available. Moreover, scrapers have benefits with regard to spreading materials evenly that only the new generation of ejector ADTs is able to match.

There are still motor scrapers in use, though many existing machines are up to 20 years old, and Cat and Terex's sales of new units are in small numbers only. The majority of sites still running these machines use two scrapers in tandem, while the remainder have either one scraper used on very short hauls or as many as three scrapers in a train for hauls of over 0.6 mile/1 kilometer.

The problem for the self-propelled scraper, though, is maintaining utilization, as there is now an insufficient number of jobs to support many fleets of these costly machines with their narrow application range. With this in mind, it is easy to understand why many contractors prefer the jack-of-all-trades solution, which relies on earthmoving fleets of ADTs and excavators (or wheel loaders). Such equipment may not be as cost efficient for a 0.6-mile/1-kilometer earthmoving job as a scraper team, but high versatility means that utilization is never likely to be a problem for ADTs and excavators.

The high purchase and running costs of motor scrapers do not apply to towed scraper boxes, though, which are comparatively cheap to buy and run. In fact, the old, heavy-duty Caterpillar towed scrapers soldier on for years because they're well built and have little to go wrong, and a number are still in use, hitched up to the back of a bulldozer. However, even these teams are comparatively rare on mining and contracting sites nowadays. It is generally considered more cost effective to use bulldozers for dozing work or sometimes for ripping rather than as tractor units.

Aware of all these factors, the team at Bell was sure its heavy-duty tractor would offer benefits that no other equipment could match at the time, with a particularly strong potential in North America, where towed scraper boxes were the most numerous. Although Bell first tested its tractor in South Africa, the North American market was understandably the firm's first target for the machine. Towed scrapers have never entirely disappeared from the North American market, and the smaller units have sold particularly well in the agricultural sector for a number of years, as farmers often hitch them up to the rear of their tractors. There was a knock-on effect, too, with a number

of these units migrating into construction and mining applications. Further aiding this market were the increasing power outputs made available in the tractor sector, with a huge growth of units offered with 400 horsepower/298 kilowatts or more.

A number of construction and mining firms spotted the cost-per-ton advantage of using these more powerful tractors to tow a scraper box rather than buying the more expensive and more specialized self-propelled scraper. However, the rise in the use of towed scraper boxes on construction and mining sites also began to highlight shortcomings in the units on the market. Built for the needs of the agricultural sector, typically with less arduous working conditions and a lower number of operating hours per month, the scraper boxes were simply not strong enough for the rigors of a construction or mine site. The same held true for the agricultural tractors used to tow the scrapers. They could do the job, but only for a while, as they were not designed to cope with the conditions in this much tougher environment or to cope with the high operating hours expected of construction and mining equipment. Bell also believed that there were questions over the suitability of these agricultural tractors for construction or mining operations due to safety requirements, particularly in regard to rollover- (ROPS) and falling-object-protection standards (FOPS).

In comparison, Bell's tractor was developed from the start with far more rugged componentry for construction and mining duty cycles. It also used the same cab as the firm's ADT, and Bell knew this met worldwide ROPS and FOPS standards, and was in line with noise and vibration limits.

Bell's tractor unit differed from anything on the market at the time of its launch because it was designed to tow a scraper box in a production application on a construction site or mining operation. And Bell knew it also tackled the problems of versatility, utilization, and cost. With no scraping work at hand, the machine could also be used to move fuel or water tankers around, as well as take on an array of other utility and service roles, such as delivering heavy truck or loader tires on-site. Bell reckoned that when its all-wheel-drive tractor was hitched to a scraper box, this combination could provide flotation characteristics superior to those of a conventional self-propelled scraper. The firm claimed this team could work in much worse underfoot conditions and could handle a steeper grade for the same reason, further extending its capabilities.

The first Bell tractor on the market was the 4206D, and its driveline had well-proven components, with the same 422-horsepower/315-kilowatt Mercedes engine and automatic Allison transmission used in the B40D ADT.

The heavy-duty front chassis section and articulation were also derived from the units developed for the B40D. There were some detail changes to the driveline components, though, with a close-ratio gearbox and some remapping of the engine's power delivery curve, while the rear chassis section was designed specifically for the tractor. While developing the 4206D, Bell's engineers also spoke at length with several manufacturers of towed scraper boxes, including Miskin and Reynolds, and a number of end users. These discussions helped Bell to optimize the tractor's specifications. Design features, such as the gearing and hitch-point arrangements in particular, required extensive consultation with the scraper box firms and end users.

According to Bell, the tractor unit that it developed was able to provide sufficient power to load up to three scrapers on a cut and then travel and dump the payload. On a tight site development project with a short area, Bell said that one scraper box would suffice, and that this would also allow a smaller turning circle. Clearly, the number of scraper boxes required for any job would be determined by the size of the work in hand. But Bell's tractor offered versatility in this regard, as a single machine could tow up to three 16.57-cubic-yard/13-cubic-meter scraper boxes without the need for another piece of equipment providing support. By comparison, conventional motor scrapers generally operate in fleets that include a dozer, while towed scraper boxes would be pulled by less-durable agricultural tractors or slower-moving bulldozers.

The first Bell tractors soon showed that even with a full load, the machines were able to haul a 42-U.S.-ton/38-tonne payload. And once Bell had evaluated the figures, the firm claimed this would be at around half the capital cost of an excavator and ADT on the same site. While its excavators and ADTs are versatile and can work in a wider array of earthmoving applications over greater distances, Bell was convinced that its tractor and towed scraper combination offered equally high utilization.

According to Bell, the numbers added up for its tractor, and as a major supplier of ADTs, the firm had a ready source of performance and cost data on the latter machines. In terms of capital investment, Bell estimated the big tractor and two scrapers would offer the same payload as a 40-U.S.-ton/36-tonne-class ADT. However, the ADT would be around 30 percent more expensive. Furthermore, the tractor and scraper could also work without an excavator or wheel loader as a loading tool, unlike the ADT (or a motor scraper and dozer team). Bell's trials showed its 4206D and scraper combination to be 50 percent more effective than a fleet of trucks and an excavator on a cost-per-ton basis to load, haul, and spread on an earthworks site with a haul distance of 437–656

yards/400–600 meters. The firm's figures also suggested a tractor and towed scraper box combination could move in the region of 510–574 cubic yards per hour/400–450 cubic meters per hour or 665–721 U.S. tons per hour/600–650 tonnes per hour on a 328-yard/300-meter haul.

Bell had worked most closely with Miskin, which had developed its heavy-duty scraper box specifically for use with the 4206D. However, there was no official joint-venture deal with Miskin, so Bell was also prepared to supply its tractors in partnership with any of the other suppliers. This even included John Deere, which has a 30 percent stake in Bell—John Deere's ADTs are in fact made by Bell.

The numbers certainly looked good. When the payload-to-empty-weight ratios and running costs were all factored in for the 4206D and scraper box combo, they were considerably better than for self-propelled scrapers. Utilization was a crucial factor, and Bell said that its 4206D could be used to haul other tow-behind implements, such as mixing plants or rear-dump trailers.

Even as the 4206D came to market, Bell decided to capitalize on the versatility of the heavy-duty tractor by offering a range of models and later introduced smaller tractors aimed at contractors in particular. Called the 2306D, the first of these units was designed for use with a 16.6-cubic-yard/13-cubic-meter scraper payload, and Bell said that machine could also haul a variety of implements, like compaction rollers, water tankers, and rear-dump trailers. Like its bigger sibling, the 2306D was based on components Bell had already proven in its ADTs, such as the Mercedes diesel and Allison transmission. Since that time Bell has added two more tractor models, the 2806D and 3806D, and now offers four machines based on its B25, B30, B35, and B40 trucks.

It was in North America that the 4206D first began to take off in terms of sales. Bell was forthright in its comments about the machine, explaining that it was successful because it was purpose-built, with a heavy-duty drivetrain, chassis, and cab. Site use soon began to affirm the high performance of this machine. Hauling 33 cubic yards/26 cubic meters per load with two scrapers, the tractor showed itself well suited to continuous bulk earthworks projects, such as overburden removal on mines. Some of the first units off Bell's production line began working in South Africa, with Trollope Mining using its machines to strip topsoil and for site rehabilitation. The 4206Ds showed themselves able to work three shifts of eight hours each, while on haul distances of 328–437 yards/300–400 meters they could handle 10 to 12 cycles per hour. Running costs were not high, as the machines consumed 7.4–7.9 U.S. gallons/28–30 liters per hour of fuel. One 4206D and scraper combination was able to take the place

A U.S. contractor converted some older Volvo ADTs to operate as tractors, and since then, Volvo has also designed a tractor unit based on one of its ADTs.

of an excavator and three ADTs, which the firm soon found provided a major reduction in comparative running costs. At the same time, the three tractors were able to move the same amount of dirt. Trials showed each 4206D could shift 4,461–5,353 cubic yards per day/3,500–4,200 cubic meters per day in general duties, increasing to some 6,373 cubic yards/5,000 cubic meters in a stockpiling application, depending on soil type.

Having supplied some of the heavy-duty scraper boxes, Miskin identified the tractor's potential for hauling other equipment. The firm then developed several towable units, including a padfoot roller and a fuel and lubrication trailer. Clearly, though, such an interesting market was not going to be left to just one manufacturer. The first sign of this was when a U.S. contractor converted a number of older Volvo ADTs to work as tractors. Volvo followed this development with interest, later unveiling its own purpose-built tractor prototype developed from the 40-U.S.-ton/36-tonne-payload A40. But it is Bell's original 4206D and later heavy-duty tractors that deserve recognition because they have used new technology to breathe new life into an old concept.

Chapter 7
LEARNING TO CRAWL
FROM TRACKED MACHINES TO AIRPLANES

It is somewhat ironic that flying machines were built long before those that could crawl. The Montgolfier brothers made the first hot-air balloon flights in 1783, with Henri Giffard's steam-driven airship flying in 1852 and the Wright brothers' heavier-than-air aeroplane in 1903. November 24, 2004, marked the 100th anniversary since Benjamin Holt, based in California, built the first successful off-highway machine running on crawler tracks, around 11 months after the Wright brothers made their initial flights. And this was around 100 years after the first steam locomotive, designed and built by Cornish mining engineer Richard Trevithic, first rattled along iron rails towing a string of coal wagons (winning Trevithic a handsome bet in doing so, as his detractors said it couldn't be done).

The impact of the crawler track should not be underestimated. This single invention was to revolutionize the earthmoving industry, increasing the efficiency of mining and construction operations ever since and laying the foundation for the U.S.$30 billion-per-year company that Caterpillar has become. The invention of the crawler track also paved the way for the bulldozer's cousin, the army tank.

Although some attempts at making track-laying machines had been tried during the nineteenth century, it was Benjamin Holt who made a design that worked. Holt developed his steam-powered machine for agricultural purposes, as he'd found that conventional traction engines running on steel wheels regularly sank up to their axles in the soft earth of California's San Joaquin Valley.

The early Holt tractors used the tiller-wheel arrangement for steering. The low-revving Cat gas/petrol engine was mounted forward of the tracks so as to place weight on the tiller wheel and help the machine to steer properly.

This restored tractor was one of the early models that did not feature a tiller wheel at the front for steering, allowing the designer to place the engine between the tracks for stability.

Large-diameter steel wheels were tried at first, but with several bolted onto one axle, the machines became incredibly wide and difficult to maneuver, making them impractical to operate. It wasn't until Holt replaced the rear wheels from the 40-horsepower/30-kilowatt Holt Junior Road Engine Number 77 tractor with crawler undercarriages that an effective low-ground-pressure solution was found. Opinion varies as to the exact dimensions of these first tracks, but some evidence suggests that they were 9 feet long by 42 inches wide and ran on pads made of 3x4-inch wooden slats. These were intended purely for use on soft earth, as wear would have been a problem for the wooden slats on stony ground. This machine featured a tiller-type front wheel for steering, a configuration that was used by Holt for some years afterward. The first unit was the product of years of development by Holt and his staff, and the firm

tinkered with the prototype for a while, making its first sale of a crawler tractor in 1906.

It was clear that more development was needed, though, as the weighty boilers the steam engines required affected performance. With power-to-weight ratios of 1,000 pounds per horsepower/608 kilograms per kilowatt, these steam-driven machines were excessively heavy and cumbersome. Further shortcomings with steam engines related to the length of time required to reach working temperatures and pressures from cold, the large crews needed to run each unit (including a skilled engineer), and the enormous quantities of coal or wood and water they consumed during operation. Recognizing that the fairly new internal combustion engine offered several benefits in terms of power-to-weight ratio, crew size, fuel consumption, and starting from cold, Benjamin Holt experimented with

Repowering an existing machine has long been a way to boost equipment performance at an economical cost. This restored Best Sixty model was repowered with one of Cat's early diesels, increasing output and reducing fuel consumption.

gasoline/petrol engines, and these were put into production in 1908. Little by little, sales of these machines grew, and Holt began making its own range of gasoline engines as a result, setting up the Aurora Engine company that is today a cornerstone of the Caterpillar group.

Holt wasn't the only person working on crawler tracks around that time, though. Working without any knowledge of Holt's development, David Roberts, chief engineer at R. Hornsby & Sons, patented the chain track in the United Kingdom in 1904. However, the Hornsby machine was not actually tested until 1905, and Holt's crawler tractor was the first to run. In fact, Hornsby built several oil- and steam-powered tractors but received little in the way of commercial interest. After supplying the British Army with a machine to test in 1911 and selling a machine to a customer in Canada for hauling coal in 1912, Hornsby sold its patent rights to Benjamin Holt in 1914 for the then-princely sum of (U.S.) $8,000. It's likely that the firm's accountants were pleased with themselves for having achieved some return from the apparently valueless chain track. Although the British military extensively tested its six-cylinder, gasoline-driven artillery tractor, concerns were expressed over having such a volatile fuel in close proximity to artillery shells, and it was decided to stick with proven horse or mule power. (The Hornsby military tractor is still in existence at the British Army's Tank Museum in Bovington.) While with the benefit of hindsight it is easy to criticize the initial short-sightedness of the British Army, it is worth noting too that German generals examined a Holt tractor immediately prior to the outbreak of the war and rejected the concept as unnecessary to their plans. So, the British generals were not alone in their lack of foresight.

With the outbreak of World War I soon after, the British military realized very quickly that horses and mules were unable to cope with the atrocious conditions and,

The Best 30 model was one of the tractors retained in the lineup when Best and Holt merged to form Caterpillar in 1925.

abandoning concerns about the fuel, turned to Holt for a supply of crawler tractors, the only machines that could operate in the terrible environment. Holt then geared up to supply the British and French war effort, building thousands of tractors for the Allies, and these units were used to haul supplies and munitions to the front lines.

It is not clear exactly who came up with the idea of mounting a steel box onto a tracked undercarriage and adding machine guns and artillery pieces to make the first armored fighting vehicle. But the British Army quickly realized the potential for this radical idea, with Winston Churchill (then in charge of the British Navy) one of its most enthusiastic supporters. Work started on this project in 1915, and it was code-named "tank" so as to deceive German intelligence into believing the British were working on a new fuel-storage system. The first prototype, nick-named Little Willy (also in the Tank Museum, Bovington), originally featured Holt undercarriage components, but

these proved unsuitable, and purpose-built units were developed instead. So impressive were the tests with the prototype that improved designs were rushed into production. These featured longer chassis, enabling them to cross the trenches. When the tanks were first used in battle in 1916, the German defenders were horrified at this new weapon, which, after further improvements based on battle experience, proved effective.

The tank quickly became the must-have fighting tool for any modern army, even though its overall impact on World War I was limited. The French Army commissioned several designs of its own, with the Char d'Assaut Schneider and the Char d'Assaut St.-Chamond models using Holt undercarriage components. These types were not successful, as their superstructures were longer than their undercarriages, limiting a much needed rough-terrain capability. Understandably, the German Army also wanted a tank, though the Sturmpanzerwagon A7V that resulted

was rushed through development; it was overweight, slow, unstable, and unreliable, and had even less ground clearance than the unsuccessful French Char d'Assaut types. Meanwhile, the U.S. military's rather more sensible response was to ask Holt to develop a prototype tank, though this came too late to be used in battle.

During the war years and long before, too, Holt had been facing tough competition within the United States from another California firm, Best, which had also been making steam-powered machines for agriculture since the 1890s. The two companies had long been fierce rivals—even resorting to legal battles—until Best sold out to Holt in 1908. But after two years with Holt, Clarence Best (son of Daniel, who founded the firm) left to set up his own company, Best Gas Traction Company, in 1910. The rivalry began again in earnest in 1913 when the Best 75 was launched, a crawler tractor with design features not dissimilar to those on Holt machines. During World War I, Holt concentrated on supplying the war effort, allowing Best to develop its market share in the United States. The Best Sixty tractor, for example, was launched in 1919, and this model was so successful that it remained in the product line for many years.

There was little love lost between the two firms, and they continued their ferocious rivalry until 1925, when they decided to call it quits and merge, forming Caterpillar. The product lines were also merged, and the most successful models, such as the Best Sixty, continued in production, though these were now sold under the new Caterpillar name (the Sixty was available until 1931). Clarence Best became president of the newly combined firm and retired in 1951.

Also during the 1920s, the high-drive concept for crawler tractors and dozers came into being. Now marketed by Caterpillar as its dozer USP, the high-drive crawler dozer undercarriage was in fact pioneered by Cleveland Tractor, with its tiny F-type appearing in 1920. Cleveland Tractor built a range of models with high drives and pioneered differential steer on track-type tractors/bulldozers, a system now used by Caterpillar and its archrival Komatsu on larger models.

If you've ever wondered why Caterpillar calls its bulldozers track-type tractors, there is a good reason. The early crawler tractors were just that, machines aimed primarily at agricultural purposes for towing various implements. As Caterpillar's machines predate the first purpose-built

Following the merger that formed Caterpillar, its tractors initially retained the nomenclature that had been used by both Holt and Best, with the Twenty-Two powered by a 22-horsepower/16.4-kilowatt engine, for example.

Caterpillar's tractors, fitted with LeTourneau blades and cable hoist systems, were used extensively by the U.S. military in World War II for airfield construction and other duties, even under enemy fire. Bulldozers are widely considered as having had more impact toward winning the Pacific campaign for the Allies than the tank.

bulldozers, the firm has stuck with its tradition of calling these units track-type tractors. Earthmoving applications in construction or mining came later, with the first dozer blades being crude devices that were raised and lowered by hand. Dozer blades were originally retrofitted items for crawler tractors and were made by small specialist firms. LaPlant-Choate was a pioneer of the powered dozer blade, making a hydraulic raise system in 1925. It used a single hydraulic cylinder fitted behind the driver's seat, and the ram pushed down on a frame that pivoted in the center of the tractor, lifting the blade at the front. But early hydraulic systems were prone to leaks, and LaPlant-Choate's design, influential though it was, came ahead of its time and initially did not prove commercially successful. It was LeTourneau's cable-operated system, launched in 1928, that provided the earthmoving industry with the first reliable powered dozer blade. This ingenious device relied on a control unit driven from the tractor's power takeoff, and its power control unit (PCU) was available with up to four winches, each with

individual clutch and brake systems. The PCU could also be used to operate towed scrapers, in which LeTourneau was a pioneer, as well as rippers or other pieces of equipment. (During World War II, Caterpillar was to build thousands of D4 dozers, most of which were fitted with LeTourneau blades and PCUs, and many are still in existence.) Other leading specialist makers of dozer blades included Bucyrus-Erie and Baker. And to meet fast-growing demand for bulldozers, the tractor manufacturers teamed up with the suppliers of dozer blades: LeTourneau and Caterpillar; Bucyrus and International; Baker and Allis-Chalmers.

Clarence Best and the other Caterpillar executives realized it was important to build the firm by ensuring it was not wholly reliant on its track-type tractor product line. In 1928, Caterpillar made the first move to expand the product line when it bought out a Minneapolis-based firm called the Russell Grader Manufacturing Company. The firm had been making self-propelled graders since 1919 (and horse-drawn units prior to that) and had even used a 27-horsepower/20-kilowatt, 2-U.S.-ton/1.8-tonne Caterpillar tractor as the base for one of its models. With highway construction and civil engineering projects increasing in the 1930s, the grader range soon became a staple of the Caterpillar product line.

The tough off-highway application also suggested to Caterpillar's engineers that a more durable and efficient power solution was needed than could be provided by the gas/petrol engines available. In March 1928, Clarence Best met with a consulting engineer named Carl George Arthur Rosén to look into the use of a diesel engine in the Caterpillar 60 tractor. Henry Kaiser (who later founded Kaiser Aluminum) had already tried 60-horsepower/44.7-kilowatt Atlas Imperial diesels in two Caterpillar 60 tractors, but these engines were designed for stationary use and were too heavy, so the experiment had not been particularly successful. Taking a year to research the subject, Rosén bought several diesels from suppliers in the United States and Europe, including engines from Benz, Atlas, Buda, and Coho. The engines were stripped down so their components could be examined, built back up, and tested

thoroughly. None proved suitable, but the team gained sufficient experience with the compression ignition engine to develop a diesel that would meet Caterpillar's needs.

By January 1930, preliminary engineering work was complete and the first pre-combustion-chamber test engine was tested on July 3, 1930. The pre-combustion-chamber configuration was employed because oil companies had yet to start producing proper diesel fuel, and instead, the fuels consisted of distillates varying widely in composition and quality, so any engine would have to burn what was available. In addition, Rosén's previous experience in the marine market had shown that fuel systems should be nonadjustable to prevent customers trying to tweak engine performance by fiddling around with the settings. And while an overhead-cam, direct-injection engine was developed around that time, it was not put into production because of the narrow fuel range it was able to handle.

In 1931, Caterpillar set the pace in the market by introducing its first diesel-powered crawler tractor, called the Diesel Sixty-Five. It used a chassis and running gear developed from those on the original Best Sixty. With its

The versatile cable system developed originally by LeTourneau was used successfully by Caterpillar to raise and lower dozer blades for many years until improved hydraulics became available.

143

Instead of lifting a dozer blade, the versatile LeTourneau power control unit (PCU) system that Caterpillar fitted to its tractors could operate a towed scraper bowl or attachments such as rippers.

rugged and purpose-built Caterpillar engine, this machine offered greater torque and lower fuel consumption than its nearest rivals.

Caterpillar's diesel-driven machine attracted major sales, and the firm quickly began supplying other firms with engines, becoming one of the world's largest manufacturers of diesels by 1933. Seeing the growing demand for Caterpillar's diesel tractor, rival crawler tractor manufacturers were quick to respond with their own models too.

Caterpillar's D9900 diesel, launched in October 1931, produced 89 horsepower/66 kilowatts at 700 rpm and tipped the scales at 2.58 U.S. tons/3.3 tonnes. Because of the dirty, off-highway application, Caterpillar had the foresight to fit the D9900 with air-intake filters, the first diesel engine so equipped, and the prototype unit is still thought to be capable of running, though it was last powered up in the 1970s. This diesel is now exhibited in the Smithsonian Institute, alongside other U.S. technical innovations such as a Wright aeroplane and rockets developed by NASA.

One of the first two Caterpillar diesel tractors produced was bought by a California farmer named W. C.

Schuder and, after clocking 27,000 hours, this was sold to Clarence Danielson. Eventually it was purchased by a collector named Fred Heidrick, who keeps it in running condition today. In fact, many of the early Holt, Best, and Caterpillar tractors, as well as competing models from the likes of Allis-Chalmers and International), are preserved in working conditions. The United States-based Historic Construction Equipment Association (HCEA) has a substantial membership, as does the Antique Caterpillar Machine Owners Club (ACMOC), and members of these groups have restored and repaired countless older machines that would have otherwise been scrapped.

Demand began to climb despite the worldwide depression, and Caterpillar's East Peoria, Illinois, plant soon had the world's first moving assembly line for making diesel engines. Caterpillar supplied its first diesel for use by another firm in June 1932 to the Thew Shovel Company of Lorain, Ohio, using a D9900 to drive a 1.5-cubic-yard/1.2-cubic-meter cable shovel. Fitting the diesel improved the machine's power, reliability, and economy in comparison with the gasoline/petrol engines or diesels

The D11 has long been the top of Caterpillar's bulldozer line and, weighing 111 U.S. tons/100 tonnes or so, offers a performance far beyond the imagination of Benjamin Holt when he developed the crawler track.

used by Thew's rivals. As a result, other equipment manufacturers soon began fitting Caterpillar diesels on their machines as well.

The Engine Sales Group subsidiary was established in 1932, supplying both diesel and gasoline engines into an ever increasing array of applications. Sales rose steadily from 13 engines sold to 9 different original equipment manufacturers (OEM) customers in 1932 to 3,430 engines sold to 136 different OEM customers just nine years later. Originally, the engines were sold in basic form, but Caterpillar gradually introduced its Power Unit idea, comprising engine, radiator, air cleaner, and cowling on an I-beam mount.

Caterpillar's diesels were popular in the off-highway sector because they were developed originally for use in crawler tractors, which made them more durable than many of their competitors. Features such as enclosed pushrods and oil-bath air cleaners were standard on Caterpillar's engines but were rare on competing units, making these rival diesels vulnerable to dirt ingress and an increased potential for failures in rigorous off-highway duty cycles.

In 1933, Caterpillar set a record by manufacturing more diesel engines than the total U.S. diesel production for the previous year. Also in 1933, Benjamin Holt's second son, William K. Holt, established a Cat dealership in San Antonio to serve central and southern Texas that continues in business today.

However, even as the market for diesel-powered machines began to develop, the sector was hit by serious technical problems as engines began to fail after just a few hundred operating hours. Strip-downs showed that the piston rings had become stuck in their grooves thanks to an accumulation of sludge, affecting compression and power output. Being compression-ignition engines, of course, as soon as the compression fell below the level needed for ignition, the engines stopped running. At first, no one was able to establish the reason for this problem, and the only answer was for a mechanic to take the engine apart, boil up each piston in a bucket of extremely noxious chemicals, and then scrape off the accumulated gunk. Then the cause became clear. Oil companies had changed their production processes in the early 1930s, and this had

removed naturally occurring detergents that broke down the sludge, leading to deposits that quickly built up and reduced compression. Caterpillar and Shell discussed the problem and found a detergent that could do the job effectively, reducing the time required for each strip-down. But it was a clever mechanic who came up with a practical solution. He began putting some detergent in the crankcase just prior to each scheduled oil change, and when the time came to drain the oil, the dissolved sludge dribbled out at the same time. Seeing this, Shell and other oil companies simply began putting tiny quantities of the detergent in the fuel, preventing the gunk from forming in the first place.

The Diesel Seventy-Five tractor with its 83-horsepower/62-kilowatt diesel was introduced during 1933 and was offered until 1935, when it was replaced by the first D8 model. Also in 1935, the eight-cylinder D17000 was launched—Caterpillar's first engine aimed at industrial applications rather than use in earthmoving machines. The D17000 was a stalwart of the lineup and remained in production for 20 years, being used in a vast array of applications such as to crush rock, drive boats, generate electricity, and power locomotives. To start this diesel, a small, two-cylinder gasoline/petrol pony engine was mounted above the flywheel, and many of these low-stressed and immensely long-lived D17000s remain in use even now.

With war starting again in Europe, Caterpillar was a natural choice when the U.S. military decided to develop a diesel engine for use in the M4 Sherman tank, given the firm's links with the concept. The original M4 tank design had retained the basic chassis and the proven but expensive (and thirsty) aircraft-derived radial engine from the previous M3 model. The military wondered if a diesel would offer better performance, lower maintenance, reduced fuel consumption, and even greater durability, at less cost. Responding fast to the technical challenge, Caterpillar had a supercharged diesel with a nine-cylinder radial configuration ready for testing in just six months. This developed 540 horsepower/335 kilowatts in standard trim (tests showed it could deliver as much as 875 horsepower/652 kilowatts) and was able to run on either diesel fuel or low-octane gasoline, while it offered major gains in performance, reliability, and safety.

Using a dozer to push a scraper is a conventional method for loading and an extremely efficient way to shift dirt in the right conditions, though the market for scrapers has declined in recent years and these machines are not as key to the Cat product line as in former times.

Some scrapers, such as elevating scrapers, are self-loading. These machines are efficient but have limitations with regard to the conditions in which they can be used.

However, so substantial was this engine's torque output that the standard M4's clutches and propeller shafts proved unequal to the task, and Caterpillar had to develop its own transmission. By the time testing of the Caterpillar radial diesel was complete, though, the U.S. military had decided to replace the complex aircraft-derived radial with other powerplants for the improved versions of the M4 tank. Most of the later Shermans used a simple and sturdy V-8 gas engine from Ford, as the military also had reservations about the logistics required in supplying its units with different fuels and preferred to concentrate on gasoline instead. Some M4s used twinned GM 6-71 diesels, though, while M4A6 Shermans powered by Caterpillar's

unusual supercharged diesel radial were also used by one battalion during World War II.

Also during this same period, Caterpillar made a bold move to broaden the product line by introducing a self-propelled scraper unit in 1941. This unit was used widely by the military for airfield construction and many other tasks, and featured the four-wheel DW-10 tractor unit with a 100-horsepower/75-kilowatt diesel coupled to a 10-cubic-yard/7.8-cubic-meter bowl made initially by LaPlant-Choate and by Caterpillar itself starting in 1947.

The postwar construction boom was good news for Caterpillar. Despite the large numbers of army surplus Cat D4s equipped with LeTourneau cable blades entering

A partnership with Mitsubishi Heavy Industries gave Caterpillar a strong push into the hydraulic excavator market, with the firm now holding one of the leading positions in the sector.

the market, Caterpillar's sales increased by leaps and bounds, with the trusty bulldozer at the heart of its success. And if the healthy trade in used D4s put a dent in Cat's sales of new equipment, it did no harm to the market for replacement parts.

The pressures of World War II had led to further growth in the use of diesels and numerous technical advances in engine design, and afterward Caterpillar was quick to introduce several new models. Most impressive of the new engines were the 12-cylinder, 500-horsepower/373-kilowatt D397 and 8-cylinder 300-horsepower/224-kilowatt D375, the largest mass-produced diesel engines of the period. By 1950, Caterpillar had 36 models of diesel engines ranging in output from 30 to 520 horsepower/22 to 388 kilowatts. In 1951 came the DW21 scraper, which set the pattern for the machines the firm still builds today. This two-wheel tractor unit was hitched to a cable-operated bowl with a capacity of 18 cubic yards/13.5 cubic meters, featured hydraulic articulation/steering, and remained in the product range for nine years.

During 1953, Caterpillar opted to replace the Special Engine Sales Group established 22 years before with the Industrial Engine Division, in recognition of the growing importance of this business segment. The developments in engine design continued too, and in 1957 came the six-cylinder inline D353, the first engine with a new 6.25-inch/159-millimeter bore, a configuration that stayed in production until 1990. This engine was designed to run at 1,200 rpm. Other new Cat diesels with similar design features included the V-8 D379, V-12 D398, and V-16 D399. In 1955 Caterpillar introduced turbocharging—boosting power while reducing emissions—with aftercooling coming in 1958 to lower charge air temperatures and optimize combustion. Also in 1955, the first of Cat's D9 dozers arrived, with a 286-horsepower/213-kilowatt engine initially that was later increased to 320 horsepower/239 kilowatts.

A further key addition to the Caterpillar product line came in 1959 with the launch of the first wheel loader model, the 944, which had a rigid chassis. With its all-wheel-drive, 100-horsepower/75-kilowatt diesel and

Crawler excavators are versatile machines and are commonly used for rock-breaking duties when fitted with hydraulic hammers, while they can also handle other attachments such as drilling equipment.

2-cubic-yard/1.6-cubic-meter bucket, the 944 was a useful performer. It was followed in 1960 by the smaller 922 and larger 966A, which shared the rigid frame configuration. The product-line expansion continued in 1962 with the launch of the 769, the firm's first true off-highway truck, which was aimed at quarrying and mining customers and was to set a pattern for the firm's rigid truck line. Coming in 1960, Caterpillar's first 600-series scrapers began replacing the earlier DW models, starting with the 619 with an 18-cubic-yard/14-cubic-meter bowl and followed by a range of other sizes. Biggest of all was the mighty 666, which had twinned engines delivering 980 horsepower/730 kilowatts and a 54-cubic-yard/42.4-cubic-meter bowl, making it the largest scraper Caterpillar ever built. In modified 666B form, it was available until 1978.

By 1963, Caterpillar was making moves to boost its wheel loader line with the introduction of its first true articulated model, the 988A, with a 6-cubic-yard/4.7-cubic-meter bucket and 325-horsepower/242-kilowatt engine. Although the 944 and 966A loaders and the

uprated 922B were to stay in production until the late 1960s, the firm concentrated on developing articulated models after the introduction of the first 988. (Caterpillar was not to offer rigid-frame loaders again until its compact skid steer loaders, based on a very different concept, appeared in the late 1990s.)

The firm's first elevating scraper made its debut in 1964. Although this line has remained a niche product, the firm still offers a range today.

During the 1960s, Caterpillar further broadened its dump truck line, though the diesel-electric models developed by Ralph Kress did not prove successful and were cut from the line. Caterpillar's subsequent truck development concentrated on mechanical-drive technology, a concept the firm believed to be superior in terms of reliability.

The hydraulic excavator market was already well developed when Caterpillar introduced its first model, the 225, in 1972. These machines had been pioneered by the Italian Bruneri brothers after World War II. European, U.S., and Japanese manufacturers had all developed

A need for a higher-mobility excavator prompted Caterpillar to turn to German expertise. Its current wheeled excavators have been developed largely in Germany, although they share features and technology with the company's crawler excavators.

designs, with German firm Demag building the crawler-based machine in the early 1950s that set the pattern for further development and the hydraulic excavator as we know it today. During the period from 1973 to 1976, Caterpillar broadened its line of crawler excavators, rolling out the 235, 245, and then the smaller 215. The company also began capitalizing on its existing relations with Mitsubishi Heavy Industries in Japan, setting up a joint venture to design, develop, market, and manufacture excavators—a relationship that still forms a cornerstone of Caterpillar today. To further develop its presence in the excavator sector, the key component in the worldwide earthmoving equipment industry, Caterpillar later established links with the German manufacturers Eder and Sennebogen to produce wheeled excavators.

Major programs of road construction got underway in many countries during the 1970s, resulting in strong sales of many machines. The motor scraper was extremely popular, and Caterpillar's models sold well during this period, as did the many other brands available at the time. However,

evidence that the market was about to change came when the U.K. company DJB began putting together articulated trucks using Caterpillar engines, transmissions, and axles. The initial reaction within Caterpillar to the emergence of these machines was not exactly favorable, as they were regarded as potential competition for the scraper line and the smaller rigid trucks. However, tempers soon cooled and discussions then started, with an agreement being drawn up with DJB's charismatic owner, David Brown. This eventually resulted in DJB building ADTs under license for Caterpillar, with these machines initially available in DJB branding as well. This was a momentous and extremely valuable turning point for Caterpillar, though no one knew it at the time, as the market for the scraper peaked in the 1970s and was never to recover. The more versatile ADT and hydraulic excavator combination was soon to grow in importance at the expense of the less flexible scrapers (though scrapers are more efficient in the right duty cycle).

The innovations continued during the 1970s with the introduction of the 85-U.S.-ton/77-tonne-payload 777

Introduced in the early 1990s, the 994 loader has been a major success for Caterpillar's mining division, with sales well surpassing the firm's initial expectations.

truck in 1977 and the D10 dozer, with Caterpillar's first high-drive track design in 1978. These two machines had a particular impact on the mining sector—the 777 because it was a true mine-sized truck for the operations of the time, and the D10 because it was an innovative approach aimed at improving productivity. Although the high-drive system was not a new concept, Caterpillar had been working it for its dozers since the late 1960s with the intention of reducing shocks from poor ground conditions through the cushioning effect of the tracks, rather than transferring the shocks to the drive axle. Weighing in at 96 U.S. tons/86.5 tonnes and with its 700-horsepower/522-kilowatt diesel and 18-foot/5.5-meter-wide blade, the D10 was the biggest bulldozer Caterpillar had ever built, and despite its size, over 1,000 were to roll off the line before the model was replaced.

In the 1980s, the mining industry was an important target for Caterpillar. The wraps came off an even bigger bulldozer, the D11, in 1986, and this weighed nearly 111 U.S. tons/100 tonnes and had a 770-horsepower/574-kilowatt diesel and a 18.4-foot/5.6-meter-wide blade. Progressive development of the truck line was also underway, and Caterpillar's 150-U.S.-ton/135-tonne 785

truck of 1985 was followed by the 190-U.S.-ton/177-tonne 789 model in 1988. Both proved highly successful. Construction remained one of Caterpillar's key markets, and the firm opted to move downward in equipment size, launching several more compact machines aimed at volume markets. The 416, Cat's first backhoe loader, appeared in 1986. Although this model found it tough to gain a foothold at first against strong competition from more established products made by rival firms like Case, JCB, and John Deere, Caterpillar soon began to capture a healthy slice of the market. The company also bought out French firm Albaret, a maker of road rollers and other similar products, around the same time. Caterpillar identified a broader range of equipment to meet miners' needs, so as to be able to offer its customers a full line of product solutions. At the start of the 1990s, Caterpillar rolled out a number of key large machines aimed specifically at the mining equipment market. The firm also introduced its 300-series excavators for the construction industry, developed in partnership with Mitsubishi Heavy Industries— machines that underpinned Caterpillar's already strong position in the sector. Thus, Caterpillar took a leading slot alongside Hitachi and Komatsu in the crucial hydraulic excavator market. For miners, the 793 truck was a logical evolution of Cat's mechanical-drive truck range, offering a 240-U.S.-ton/217-tonne payload and competing with the Haulpak 830E also emerging at that time, as well as the earlier Wiseda KL-2450. The 196-U.S.-ton/177-tonne 994 wheel loader was the largest such machine Caterpillar had ever built. Though bigger loaders had been offered by other manufacturers, this was a radical departure for Caterpillar. With its 1,230-horsepower/932-kilowatt 12.75–38.2-cubic-yard/10–30-cubic-meter buckets, depending on application, the 994 weighed some 100 U.S. tons/90 tonnes more than the firm's previous top-of-the-line loader, the 992D. The 5130 mining shovel had a 755-horsepower/563-kilowatt diesel, 13.4-cubic-yard/10.5-cubic-meter bucket, and weighed in at 194 U.S. tons/175 tonnes, over 116.4 U.S. tons/105 tonnes more than the 245B shovel that had topped the line not long before. The 5130 shovel was then followed into the market by the top-of-the-line 5230, weighing in at 349 U.S. tons/315 tonnes, wielding a 21.67-cubic-yard/17-cubic-meter bucket and powered by a 1,468-horsepower/1,095-kilowatt diesel. Since that time, the 793 has gone on to become the biggest-selling large mine truck on the market, while sales of the 994 loader (and

the subsequent 994D and recent 994F) far exceeded Caterpillar's expectations for what it had first assumed would be a relatively niche product.

The 1996 MINExpo show saw the unveiling of an innovative large loader design, Caterpillar's 992G, as well as the huge 24H grader, the biggest the firm had ever made. With its striking single-arm front end, the 992G was in many respects an even more radical concept than its larger (yet more conventional) stablemate, the 994. After final product testing and tweaking had been carried out, the 992G was made available in 1997, and customers were able to run the machine in the dirt for real. The advantage of the cast single-arm front end was that it was around 30 percent lighter than the conventional twin-arm configuration, allowing the Cat engineers to give the 992G a little more reach and bucket payload than would have otherwise been achievable.

The 24H grader was developed to meet demands from miners for a larger machine capable of maintaining haul roads for big mine trucks. Although it was built on conventional design principles, the 69-U.S.-ton/62-tonne 24H was nonetheless a major innovation, with its 24-foot/7.3-meter-wide blade and 500-horsepower/373-kilowatt engine.

The success of Caterpillar's 789 and 793 trucks has made these models the backbone of its mining equipment division. The firm's competitors often regard the 789 and 793 as the machines to beat.

The Caterpillar 992G loader, first seen in public in 1996 and introduced in 1997, featured a radical, one-piece boom that was lighter than the twin booms used on the previous model, giving it greater reach and a bigger bucket capacity.

Meanwhile, launched at the same time as the 992G loader, the 790 wheeled dozer from Australian firm Tiger Engineering used the basic chassis, cab, and drivetrain from the 992G. Tiger had been building wheeled dozers using components from Cat's wheel loader machines for some years with full approval from the firm. However, soon after the launch of the 790, Caterpillar decided to buy the design rights to the wheeled models from Tiger and incorporate them into the Cat product line. The 790 became Caterpillar's 854G, while the slightly smaller 690 became the 844.

Buying the wheeled dozer models from Tiger was one of several similar moves Caterpillar made at that time, as the firm announced it would buy the factory making the Caterpillar-branded ADTs and telehandlers along with the design rights to these machines from DJB. Caterpillar also announced its intention to acquire 100 percent of the Australia-based Elphinstone product line, which had been making very successful underground loaders and trucks based around Cat components (again with full approval) for some years.

More technical innovations for the mining market were to come, and in 1997, Caterpillar silenced many industry rumors when it rolled out its giant 797 truck, aimed primarily at Canada's expanding tar sands operations. With power from a purpose-built 24-cylinder engine developed from two 3512s bolted crankshaft to crankshaft and featuring Cat's trademark mechanical drive and a payload of 360 U.S. tons/325 tonnes, the 797 was the firm's answer to demands for ever larger truck capacities. With the onset of the twenty-first century, the innovations continued, and upgraded as the 797B, the machine was to offer a 380-U.S.-ton/345-tonne payload, a top speed of 423 miles per hour/68 kilometers per hour, and a gross power of 3,550 horsepower/2,647 kilowatts from its improved 3524B diesel. The firm also announced the first of its ACERT diesel engines, featuring advanced technology designed to meet new targets for reduced noise and exhaust emissions. The sophistication of these diesels, with features such as electronically controlled high-pressure fuel injection, four valve heads with crossflow technology, and efficient turbocharging and cooling, represented a quantum leap over the previous generation of engines from the

Caterpillar's 988 loader is another machine that features the one-piece boom configuration. The design allows for better forward visibility according to the firm, as there is a better field of view to either side of the boom assembly.

In recent years, Caterpillar has moved into the road-machinery market through acquisitions such as the Italian company Bitelli, adding lines of asphalt pavers, rollers, and planers.

The 5130B mining excavator replaced the earlier 5130, which had been the first of Caterpillar's heavy hydraulic shovel/backhoe models.

firm. Power-to-weight ratios had increased substantially, with the 3524B weighing around 11 U.S. tons/10 tonnes and generating 3,550 horsepower/2,647 kilowatts, compared with the 3.7-U.S.-tons/3.3-tonne D9900 diesel of 1931, which delivered just 89 horsepower/66 kilowatts. Using these figures, the 3524B delivered 1.34 horsepower/1 kilowatt for each 8.4 pounds/3.8 kilograms or so that the engine weighs, while the D9900 was able to produce 1.34 horsepower/1 kilowatt for each 110 pounds/50 kilograms.

The 5000-series model line that had started with the 5130 and followed with the 5230 was rounded out in 2001 by the 138-U.S.-ton/125-tonne 5110B (the 5110 was never launched). But despite its promise, this machine was only ever available in backhoe form. The fact that a shovel version of the 5110B was not offered was a sign of what was to come. After over 10 years of fighting tough competition in the hydraulic mining shovel market, Caterpillar decided its rivals in the sector—Hitachi, Komatsu, Liebherr, and Terex O&K—were too strong and made the tough decision to axe the 5000 series.

However, the development continues, and more new designs are being worked on every day within the Caterpillar organization, ranging from compact construction machines right up to large pieces of mining equipment. The range of applications for these mobile machines is equally diverse, with duties encompassing virtually all major sectors of the construction and mining industries. Caterpillar continues to be a leader in engineering innovation, with leading-edge technologies in areas such as software, hydraulics, electronics, combustion, fuel injection, and good old mechanical engineering.

Since Benjamin Holt developed the crawler track, many changes have occurred in the earthmoving equipment market. But the crawler tractor remains a core product in the Caterpillar line, and its powerful and successful D11 continues to top a range that is constantly being updated and improved. The Holt name (and family) also continues its link with Caterpillar, through the Texas-based dealership Holt Cat run by CEO Peter M. Holt, great-grandson of Benjamin Holt.

Caterpillar offers a line of wheeled dozers that utilize modified drivetrains and chassis units from the wheel loaders and blades from the crawler dozers.

The Caterpillar water tankers use standard chassis from the smaller rigid truck models fitted with large water tanks and spray equipment and are used for dust suppression on-site.

REFERENCES

Chapters 1–7: *Giant Earthmovers* by Keith Haddock; *Faszination Baumaschinen* by Heinz-Herbert Cohrs; *The LeTourneau Legend* by Philip Gowenlock; corporate websites for BelAZ, Caterpillar, Hitachi, Komatsu, and Liebherr; The Tank Museum, Bovington, England.

INDEX

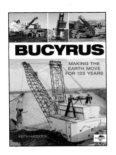

**Bucyrus:
Making the Earth Move
for 125 Years**
ISBN 0-7603-2286-4

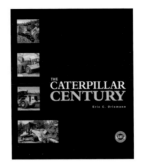

The Caterpillar Century
ISBN 0-7603-1604-X

Building Giant Earthmovers
ISBN 0-7603-0640-0

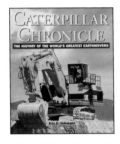

**Caterpillar Chronicle:
History of the World's
Greatest Earthmovers**
ISBN 0-7603-0667-2

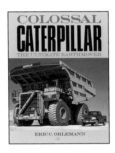

**Colossal Caterpillar:
The Ultimate Earthmover**
ISBN 0-7603-0874-8

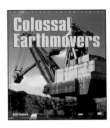

Colossal Earthmovers
ISBN 0-7603-0771-7

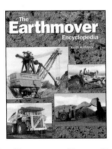

The Earthmover Encyclopedia
ISBN 0-7603-1405-5

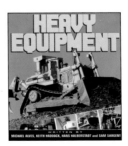

Heavy Equipment
ISBN 0-7603-1775-5

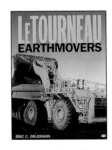

LeTourneau Earthmovers
ISBN 0-7603-0840-3

ULTRA HAULERS

GLOBAL GIANTS OF THE MINING

MIKE WOOF

LIEBHERR
Ti 272

MBI

Dedication

To my wife, Petra, who encouraged me with this project, and to my two sons, Otto and Tom.

First published in 2006 by MBI, an imprint of MBI Publishing Company, Galtier Plaza, Suite 200, 380 Jackson Street, St. Paul, MN 55101-3885 USA

MBI titles are also available at discounts in bulk quantity for industrial or sales-promotional use. For details write to Special Sales Manager at MBI Publishing Company, Galtier Plaza, Suite 200, 380 Jackson Street, St. Paul, MN 55101-3885 USA.

ISBN-13: 978-0-7603-2381-6
ISBN-10: 0-7603-2381-X

Editors: Lindsay Hitch and Steve Gansen
Designer: Kou Lor

Printed in China

On the front cover: The Caterpillar 992G loader, first seen in public in 1996 and introduced in 1997, featured a radical, one-piece boom that was lighter than the twin booms used on the previous model, giving it greater reach and a bigger bucket capacity.

On the frontispiece: The rear axle of Caterpillar's 797/797B retains the firm's trademark mechanical driveline system and features a huge differential. Although it is large, this differential follows the same basic design principles as seen in the firm's first haul truck, the 769, launched in the early 1960s.

On the title page: The TI272 represents a radical departure from established design convention, and its layout may well provide a solution for larger payloads, as well as ways to reduce haulage costs for the smaller capacities of existing truck classes. *Liebherr collection*

On the back cover: Unit Rig's MT3300 was one of the first trucks to be offered with the MTU4000-series engine and was later the first mine truck outside of the ultra hauler class to be offered with AC drive. **Inset:** Aveling Barford's rigid trucks first appeared in the 1950s and were developed continuously, proving particularly successful in the U.K. quarrying sector. The RD65 was the top-of-the-range machine, with a planned 85 tonner never progressing further than its chassis construction.

About the author:
Mike Woof has a background in mechanical engineering and wrote numerous articles as editor of *World Mining Equipment*, focusing on mining equipment and technology from the exploration stage through material processing. He then served  as international editor for *E&MJ* and *Coal Age*, and is now editor of *World Highways* magazine based near London.